D1140898

TEDBooks

The Terrorist's Son

A Story of Choice

BY ZAK EBRAHIM
WITH JEFF GILES

TED Books
Simon & Schuster

London   New York   Toronto   Sydney   New Delhi

TEDBooks

First published in Great Britain by Simon & Schuster UK Ltd, 2014
A CBS COMPANY

First TED Books hardcover edition September 2014

TED, the TED logo, and TED Books are trademarks of TED Conferences, LLC.

For information on licensing the TED talk that accompanies this book,
or other content partnerships with TED, please contact TEDBooks@TED.com.

3 5 7 9 10 8 6 4 2

Simon & Schuster UK Ltd
1st Floor
222 Gray's Inn Road
London WC1X 8HB

www.simonandschuster.co.uk

Simon & Schuster Australia, Sydney
Simon & Schuster India, New Delhi

A CIP catalogue record for this book
is available from the British Library

ISBN: 978-1-47113-906-2
ISBN: 978-1-47113-907-9 (ebook)

Interior design by MGMT
Jacket Design by Lewis Csizmazia

Printed and bound by CPI Group (UK) Ltd, Croydon, CR0 4YY

A man is but a product of his thoughts.
What he thinks, he becomes.

—Gandhi

CONTENTS

The Terrorist's Son

1 November 5, 1990
Cliffside Park, New Jersey

My mother shakes me awake in my bed: "There's been an accident," she says.

I am seven years old, a chubby kid in Teenage Mutant Ninja Turtle pajamas. I'm accustomed to being roused before dawn, but only by my father, and only to pray on my little rug with the minarets. Never by my mother.

It's eleven at night. My father is not home. Lately, he has been staying at the mosque in Jersey City deeper and deeper into the night. But he is still Baba to me— funny, loving, warm. Just this morning he tried to teach me, yet again, how to tie my shoes. Has he been in an accident? What *kind* of accident? Is he hurt? Is he *dead*? I can't get the questions out because I'm too scared of the answers.

My mother flings open a white sheet—it mushrooms briefly, like a cloud—then leans down to spread it on the floor. "Look in my eyes, Z," she says, her face so knotted with worry that I hardly recognize her. "You need to get dressed as quick as you can. And then you need to put your things onto this sheet, and wrap it up tight. Okay? Your sister will help you." She moves toward the door. "*Yulla*, Z, *yulla*. Let's go."

"Wait," I say. It's the first word I've managed to utter

since I tumbled out from under my He-Man blanket. "What should I put in the sheet? What . . . *things*?"

I'm a good kid. Shy. Obedient. I want to do as my mother says.

She stops to look at me. "Whatever will fit," she says. "I don't know if we're coming back."

She turns, and she's gone.

Once we've packed, my sister, my brother, and I pad down to the living room. My mother has called my father's cousin in Brooklyn—we call him Uncle Ibrahim, or just Ammu—and she's talking to him heatedly now. Her face is flushed. She's clutching the phone with her left hand and, with her right, nervously adjusting her *hijab* where it's come loose around her ear. The TV plays in the background. Breaking news. *We interrupt this program*. My mother catches us watching, and hurries to turn it off.

She talks to Ammu Ibrahim awhile longer, her back to us. When she hangs up, the phone begins ringing. It's a jarring sound in the middle of the night: too loud and like it *knows* something.

My mother answers. It is one of Baba's friends from the mosque, a taxi driver named Mahmoud. Everyone calls him Red because of his hair. Red sounds desperate to reach my father. "He's not here," my mother says. She listens for a moment. "Okay," she says, and hangs up.

The phone rings again. That terrible noise.

This time, I can't figure out who's calling. My mother says, "Really?" She says, "Asking about us? The police?"

A little later, I wake up on a blanket on the living room floor. Somehow, in the midst of the chaos, I've nodded off. Everything we could possibly carry—and more—is piled by the door, threatening to topple at any second. My mother paces around, checking and rechecking her purse. She has all of our birth certificates: proof, if anyone demands it, that she is our mother. My father, El-Sayyid Nosair, was born in Egypt. But my mother was born in Pittsburgh. Before she recited the Shahada in a local mosque and became a Muslim—before she took the name Khadija Nosair—she went by Karen Mills.

"Your Uncle Ibrahim is coming for us," she tells me when she sees me sitting up and rubbing my eyes. The worry in her voice is tinged with impatience now. "If he ever gets here."

I do not ask where we are going, and no one tells me. We just wait. We wait far longer than it should take Ammu to drive from Brooklyn to New Jersey. And the longer we wait, the faster my mother paces and the more I feel like something in my chest is going to burst. My sister puts an arm around me. I try to be brave. I put an arm around my brother.

"Ya Allah!" my mother says. "This is making me insane."

I nod like I understand.

• • •

Here is what my mother is not saying: Meir Kahane, a militant rabbi and the founder of the Jewish Defense

League, has been shot by an Arab gunman after a speech in a ballroom at a Marriott hotel in New York City. The gunman fled the scene, shooting an elderly man in the leg in the process. He rushed into a cab that was waiting in front of the hotel, but then bolted out again and began running down the street, gun in hand. A law enforcement officer from the U.S. Postal Service, who happened to be passing by, exchanged fire with him. The gunman collapsed on the street. The newscasters couldn't help noting a gruesome detail: both Rabbi Kahane and the assassin had been shot in the neck. Neither was expected to live.

Now, the TV stations are updating the story constantly. An hour ago, while my sister, brother, and I slept away the last seconds we had of anything remotely resembling a childhood, my mother overheard the name Meir Kahane and looked up at the screen. The first thing she saw was footage of the Arab gunman, and her heart nearly stopped: it was my father.

• • •

It's one in the morning by the time Uncle Ibrahim pulls up in front of our apartment. He has taken so long because he waited for his wife and children to get ready. He insisted they accompany him because, as a devout Muslim, he couldn't risk being alone in a car with a woman who was not his wife—my mother, in other words. There are five people in the car already. And there are four more of us trying to wedge in somehow. I feel my mother's anger rise: She's just as devout as my uncle, but *her* children were going to be in the car with the two of them anyway, so what was the point of wasting all that time?

Soon, we are driving through a tunnel, the sickly fluorescent lights rushing over our heads. The car is crazily cramped. We're a giant knot of legs and arms. My mother needs to use the bathroom. Uncle Ibrahim asks if she wants to stop somewhere. She shakes her head. She says, "Let's just get the kids to Brooklyn and then let's go to the hospital. Okay? Quick as we can. *Yulla*."

It's the first time anyone has used the word *hospital*. My father is in the hospital. Because he's had an *accident*. That means he is hurt, but it also means he is not dead. The pieces of the puzzle start clicking together in my head.

When we get to Brooklyn—Ammu Ibrahim lives in a vast brick apartment building near Prospect Park—all nine of us fall out of the car in a tangled lump. Once we're in the lobby, the elevator takes forever to come, so my mother, desperate for the bathroom, takes my hand and whisks me toward the staircase.

She takes the steps two at a time. I struggle to keep up. I see the second floor blur by, then the third. Ammu's apartment is on the fourth. We're panting as we round the corner to his hallway. We're ecstatic that we've made it—we've beaten the elevator! And then we see three men in front of my uncle's door. Two are wearing dark suits and walking toward us slowly, their badges held high. The other man is a police officer, and he's gripping his gun in its holster. My mother walks toward them. "I have to go to the bathroom," she says, "and I will talk to you when I'm done."

The men look confused, but they let her go. It's only when she tries to bring me into the bathroom too that one of the dark suits puts his palm in the air, like a traffic cop.

"The boy has to stay with us," he says.

"He's my son," she tells them. "He's coming with me."

"We can't allow it," says the other dark suit.

My mother is puzzled, but only for a moment: "You think I'm going to hurt myself in there? You think I'm going to hurt my *son*?"

The first suit looks at her blankly. "The boy stays with us," he says. Then he looks down at me with a poor attempt at a smile. "You must be"—he checks his notebook—"Abdulaziz?"

Terrified, I start nodding and can't stop. "Z," I say.

Ibrahim's family comes through the apartment door now and breaks the awkward silence. His wife herds the children into the apartment's one bedroom and commands us to sleep. There are six of us. There's a colorful matrix of bunks for kids built into the wall, like something you'd see at the PlayPlace at McDonald's. We lie in every available cranny, writhing like worms, while my mother talks to the police in the living room. I strain to listen through the wall. All I can hear are low grunts and furniture scratching against the floor.

• • •

In the living room, the dark suits have so many questions that it's like my mother is caught in a hailstorm. She will remember two questions above all others: What is your current home address? And, Did you know your husband was going to shoot Rabbi Kahane tonight?

The answer to the first is more complicated than the answer to the second.

Baba works for the City of New York, repairing the heat and air-conditioning in a Manhattan courthouse, and the city requires that its employees live in one of the five boroughs. So we pretend to live in my uncle's apartment. The police only showed up here tonight because of that little lie in the record books.

My mother explains all this. And she tells the policemen the truth about the shooting: She'd known nothing about it. She hadn't heard a single syllable. *Nothing.* She abhors talk of violence. Everyone at the mosque knows better than to agitate in her presence.

She answers a barrage of follow-up questions, head high, hands motionless on her lap. But all the while one thought is banging inside her head like a migraine: She must go to my father. She must be at his side.

Finally, my mother blurts out: "I heard on TV that Sayyid is going to die."

The dark suits look at each other, but do not answer.

"I want to be with him. I don't want him to die alone."

Still no answer.

"Will you take me to him? Please? Will you take me to him, *please*?"

She says it again and again. Eventually the dark suits sigh and put away their pencils.

• • •

Police are swarming everywhere in front of the hospital. There is a rowdy crowd assembling of the angry, the frightened, and the curious. There are TV vans and satellite trucks. A helicopter overhead. My mother and Ibrahim are handed off to a pair of uniformed policemen who are openly hostile. My family is nothing to them. *Less* than nothing: the family of an assassin. My mother is shell-shocked and dizzy and, of all things, starving. The policemen's anger is just one more thing she senses as if through a cloudy pane of glass.

She and Ibrahim are brought in through an entrance at the far end of the hospital. On the way to the elevators, my mother peers down a long hallway, freshly waxed and gleaming under the stark lights. She sees a mass of people clamoring to get through security. Reporters are shouting questions. Cameras are flashing. My mother feels clammy and weak. Her head, her stomach, everything starts to rebel.

"I'm going to fall," she tells Ibrahim. "Can I hold on to you?"

Ibrahim balks. As a devout Muslim, he's not permitted to touch her. He allows her to hang on to his belt.

At the elevator bank, one of the policemen points and says gruffly, *"Get in."* They ride up to intensive care in hostile silence. When the elevator opens, my mother steps into the bright light of the ICU. A SWAT officer jumps to attention and levels his rifle at her chest.

She gasps. Ibrahim gasps. One of the policemen rolls his eyes and waves the SWAT officer off. He lowers his gun.

My mother rushes to my father's bed. Ibrahim drifts in slowly behind her to give her space.

Baba is unconscious, his body badly swollen and stripped to the waist. He's attached to a half-dozen machines by wires and tubes, and he's got a long, stitched-up wound on his neck from where the postal police officer shot him. It looks like there's a giant caterpillar on his neck. Nurses work hurriedly at my father's bedside. They are not happy about the interruption.

My mother reaches out to touch Baba's shoulder. His body is hard and his skin so cold that she recoils. "He's already dead?" she asks, her voice trembling. "Ya Allah, he's already dead!"

"No, he's not *dead*," one of the nurses says, not bothering to hide her annoyance. *The family of an assassin.* "And keep your hands off him. You can't touch him."

"He's my husband. Why can't I touch him?"

"Because we have rules."

My mother is too upset to understand, but later she'll decide that the nurses were afraid she would tear out the tubes and wires and let my father die. She puts her hands at her sides now. She leans down to whisper in his ear. She tells him that it's okay, that she is there beside him, that she loves him, that—if he's just been holding on for her—it's okay, she is there, she loves him, he can let go. When the nurses are not looking, she kisses his cheek.

Later, in a small conference room off the ICU, a doctor tells my mother that my father is going to live. The doctor is the first kind person she has encountered all night and—comforted by his empathy, uncomplicated and humane—she cries for the first time. He waits for her to gather herself before he says anything more. The doctor says Baba lost most of the blood in his body, and was given a transfusion. He still has a bullet somewhere in his neck but, because his carotid artery was nearly severed, they didn't want to risk probing around for it. The fact that the bullet never exited my father's body is what saved his life.

The doctor sits with my mother while she takes all this in, or tries to. Then the policemen return. They usher my mother and Ibrahim to the elevator and press the down button. When the elevator arrives and the doors open, one of them points and says again, *"Get in."*

Outside, it is dawn. On any other day, the sky would seem beautiful. But Rabbi Kahane's death has just been confirmed—the bullet did exit *his* body, so he died of the same wound that nearly killed my father—and the parking lot is still filled with police cars and satellite trucks and everything is ugly and neither my mother nor Ibrahim has been able to make their morning prayers. My mother consoles herself with two things. One is that, whatever possessed my father to commit such a monstrous act, he will never hurt anyone again. The other is that his survival is a gift.

On both counts, she is wrong.

2 Present Day

There's a reason that murderous hatred has to be taught—and not just taught, but forcibly implanted. It's not a naturally occurring phenomenon. It is a lie. It is a lie told over and over again—often to people who have no resources and who are denied alternative views of the world. It's a lie my father believed, and one he hoped to pass on to me.

• • •

What my father did on November 5, 1990, decimated my family. It tipped us into a life of death threats and media harassment, nomadic living and constant poverty, a thousand "fresh starts" that almost always led to something worse. His was an infamy of an entirely new kind, and we were collateral damage. My father was the first known Islamic jihadist to take a life on American soil. He worked with the support of a terror cell overseas that would ultimately call itself Al-Qaeda.

And his career as a terrorist was not over yet.

In early 1993, from his prison cell at Attica, my father helped plan the first bombing of the World Trade Center with his old associates from the Jersey City mosque, including Omar Abdel-Rahman, whom the media dubbed "the Blind Sheikh" and who wore a fez and Wayfarer sunglasses. On February twenty-sixth of that year, a Kuwaiti-born man named Ramzi Yousef and a Jordanian named Eyad Ismoil carried out the plot, driving a yellow Ryder van full of explosives into the parking garage below the WTC. Their horrible hope, and my father's, was that one tower would knock over the other and the death toll would be stratospheric. They had to settle for a blast that tore a hole one hundred feet wide through four levels of concrete, the injury of more than a thousand innocents, and the deaths of six people, one of them a woman seven months pregnant.

Between my mother's attempts to protect her children from the awful knowledge of their father's actions and my own little-kid desperation not to know, it would be many years before I internalized the full horror of the assassination and the bombing. It would take me just as long to admit how furious I was with my father for what he had done to my own family. At the time it was too much to take in. I carried fear, anger, and self-loathing around in my gut, but couldn't even begin to process them. I turned ten after the first World Trade Center bombing. Emotionally, I was already like a computer powering down. By the time I was twelve, I'd been bullied so much at school that I thought about suicide. It wasn't until my mid-twenties that I met a woman named Sharon who made me feel like I was worth something—and that my story was, too. It's the story of a boy trained to hate, and a man who chose a different path.

• • •

I've spent my life trying to understand what drew my father to terrorism, and struggled with the knowledge that I have his blood in my veins. By telling my story, my intention is to do something hopeful and instructive: to offer a portrait of a young man who was raised in the fires of fanaticism and embraced nonviolence instead. I can't make any grand claims for myself, but all our lives have themes, and the theme of mine so far is this: Everyone has a choice. Even if you're trained to hate, you can choose tolerance. You can choose empathy.

The fact that my father went to prison for an unfathomable crime when I was seven just about ruined my life. But it also made my life possible. He could not fill me with hate from jail. And, more than that, he could not stop me from coming in contact with the sorts of people he demonized and discovering that they were human beings—people I could care about and who could care about me. Bigotry cannot survive experience. My body rejected it.

My mother's faith in Islam never wavered during our trials as a family, but she, like the vast majority of Muslims, is anything but a zealot. When I was eighteen and had finally seen a sliver of the world, I told my mom I could no longer judge people based on *what* they were—Muslim, Jewish, Christian, gay, straight—and that starting right then and there I was only going to

judge them based on *who* they were. She listened, she
nodded, and she had the wisdom to speak the six most
empowering words I have ever heard: "I'm so tired of
hating people."

She had good reason to be tired. Our journey had been
harder on her than anyone else. For a time, she took to
wearing not only the *hijab* that hid her hair, but also the
veil called the *niqab* that cloaked everything but her eyes:
She was a devout Muslim *and* she was afraid she'd be
recognized.

Recently, I asked my mother if she knew what was
in store for our family when she walked out of Bellevue
with Ammu Ibrahim on the morning of November 6,
1990. "No," she told me, without hesitation. "I went from
being a mother with a normal life to insanity, to public
life, avoiding the media, dealing with the government,
dealing with the FBI, dealing with the police, dealing
with lawyers, dealing with Muslim activists. It was like a
line was crossed. I stepped over it and went from one life
to another. I had no idea how difficult it would be."

My father is now in the United States penitentiary
in Marion, Illinois, having been sentenced to life plus
fifteen years with no chance of parole for, among
other things, seditious conspiracy, murder in aid of
racketeering, attempted murder of a postal officer, use
of a firearm in the commission of a murder, use of a
firearm during an attempted murder, and possession
of a firearm. To be honest, I still feel *something* for him,
something that I haven't been able to eradicate—some

strand of pity and guilt, I guess, though it's thin as spider's silk. It's hard to think of the man I once called Baba living in a cell, knowing that we have all changed our names out of terror and shame.

I have not visited my father in twenty years. This is the story of why.

3 1981
Pittsburgh, Pennsylvania

Years before she meets my father, my mother falls in love with an atheist.

She has been raised by my grandmother, a devoted Christian and an even more devoted smoker, who sends her to Catholic school and supports her family by working for Bell Atlantic for decades. My mother has never known her father because he abandoned his family when she was a kid.

My mother's a serious Catholic, but there's so much that she loves and admires about the atheist that she marries him anyway. The union lasts long enough to yield a child, my sister. Eventually, though, she realizes that she can't raise a child with a man who mocks religion.

The marriage collapses. Then, unexpectedly, her faith in Catholicism does, too. She's gone to a priest for advice about some passing matter—she's known him since grade school—and the discussion has drifted to theology. My mother believes in the Holy Trinity, but admits to the priest that she's never actually *understood* it. The priest begins to explain. However, the more questions my mother asks—the hungrier she gets for clarity—the more knotted and unsatisfying his answers become. The priest gets flustered, then angry. My mother hadn't meant to be combative. She tries to defuse the situation. It's too late. "If you have to ask all these questions," the priest scolds her, "then you have no faith at all!"

My mother is dumbstruck. "I felt as if he'd stabbed me in the heart," she'll tell me decades later. Her faith in God is not shaken, but she knows, even as she leaves the rectory, that she is no longer a Catholic. My mother is still in her twenties—divorced now, and studying to be a teacher. She takes her two-year-old daughter and ventures off in search of a new religion to pour her faith into, as well as a new husband.

Early on in her quest, my mother finds a book about Islam on the shelf of a Pittsburgh library. She visits a local mosque, or *masjid,* to ask questions, and meets Muslim college students from Afghanistan and Egypt, from Libya and Saudi Arabia—from everywhere. She had no idea how warm and family-centric the community was. The men, in particular, are nothing like the standoffish, coldly masculine Muslim stereotype. They wave happily to my sister as she toddles around.

In 1982, toward the end of May, my mother sits in a study room upstairs at the mosque. She is about to convert to Islam and has been practicing the Shahada: *There is no god but God, and Muhammad is his messenger.* The creed must be spoken in earnest. It must be cleansed of all doubt and radiate only love and submissiveness. In the back of my mother's mind, like static on a radio station, she hears the disapproving voice of her own mother, who's appalled that she has been lured into Islam and has told her that she'll never be welcome in her house wearing some goddamn scarf around her head. She has literally used the words "What will the neighbors think?"

My mother pushes the negativity away. Her faith in Islam, her *need* for it, is already deep and strong. She repeats the Shahada under her breath, over and over, until it reflects what she feels in her heart: *There is no god but God, and Muhammad is his messenger. There is no god but God . . .*

She is interrupted by Hani, a new friend from the *masjid*. Hani has been helping my mother on her journey to Islam. He tells her that there's a men's prayer circle in the mosque at the moment and they would be honored if my mother would recite the Shahada in front of them— and become a Muslim in their presence.

My mother's nerves are already in a knot, and her cheeks bloom red at the thought.

Hani rushes to explain: "It won't be scary, or I wouldn't ask. But they love to watch people convert." He does not add that watching *her* convert might be of particular interest.

"Sarah said she'd sit next to you," Hani says. "If it makes you more comfortable?"

My mother consents against her better judgment. Hani tells her she'll be a huge hit, and she responds by testing out one of her new Arabic phrases: "Inshallah." *God willing.* Hani loves it. He beams as he closes the door.

Downstairs, my mother squeezes her friend Sarah's hand in solidarity, and then—drawing a deep breath as if she's diving into the ocean—walks into the mosque. Fittingly, the carpet is the blue-green of waves in sunlight. The walls are decorated with a dense, starry pattern of deep red and gold. The men in the prayer circle are seated on the rug. Some of them wear conventional Western clothing: slacks, even jeans, and button-down shirts. Others wear long, billowy shirts that hang below their knees and round, white skullcaps with needlework in blue and gold. My mother realizes that she knows the word for that sort of cap—*taqiyah*—and she repeats it in her head to calm down. The prayer circle falls silent. They turn to watch the women approach. For a few agonizing moments, the only sound is my mother's whispering and Sarah's socks on the rug. *Taqiyah,* my mother thinks. *Taqiyah, taqiyah, taqiyah.*

She recites the Shahada flawlessly, if in a quavering tone. Only then does her body finally start to relax. Her breathing grows slow and steady again. And, without thinking about whether it's proper, she steals a look at the men in the room. Her first act as a Muslim! She's a little ashamed, yes. *And yet.* One of the men is quite handsome: *he looks like an ancient Egyptian in a painting*, she thinks. She lingers half an instant too long over his bright green eyes.

Two days later, Hani tells my mother that a man from the prayer circle is interested in her and would like to meet her. There is no dating in Islam—*When a man and a woman are alone together,* the Prophet has warned, *the third person among them is Satan*—so this can only mean he wants to marry her. Marry her! Having heard her utter no more than a dozen words! Hani assures her that the man is a friend. His name is Sayyid Nosair. He is Egyptian. Could he be the Man with the Eyes? She tries to force the thought from her mind.

Within the week, my mother meets Sayyid for the first time at the home of a Libyan couple named Omar and Rihan. Omar has been acting as her guardian because she has no real relationship with either of her parents. He has already initiated the marriage machinery: He's met with Sayyid, made inquiries about him within the community, and satisfied himself that he is a good Muslim, that he's active at the *masjid* and attends as many prayer services as he can. Now Rihan is placing a tray on the coffee table in the living room— hibiscus juice, baklava, shortbread biscuits dusted with sugar and stuffed with dates—and Sayyid is knocking on the door.

Omar goes to the door, and Rihan scurries off to get a look at the visitor. My mother sits nervously on the couch. She hears Omar and Sayyid offer each other peace: her guardian saying, *"Asalaam alaykum,"* her suitor responding more generously than is necessary, *"Wa alaykum assalam wa rahmatu Allah."* He is trying to make a good impression, my mother thinks. She smiles to herself, a passage from the Qur'an fresh in her memory: *When a greeting is offered, you answer it with an even better greeting, or (at least) with its like. Allah keeps account of all things.*

Rihan scurries back into the living room ahead of the men—she's more nervous than my mother—and adjusts the cookies. "So *handsome*," she whispers. "And such green-green eyes!"

Within two minutes of sitting down with my mother, my father says shyly, "I guess you know I'm here to talk about marriage."

In Egypt, my father studied engineering and industrial design, specializing in metals. He is creative. He can design a ship as easily as a necklace. Though he has been in the States less than a year, he's found a job at a jeweler's, where—a few days after meeting my mother—he draws and casts an engagement ring. He spares no expense. The ring is beautiful and heavy. When my mother sees it, her eyes go wide.

• • •

My parents marry on June 5, 1982, ten days after meeting for the first time. Such a short courtship sounds ominous, I know—like the prelude to what could only be a tragedy. But the Western world's routine of sex, love, and marriage—which generally arrive in that order—has yielded its share of misery and divorce. Isn't it possible that some other set of rituals and expectations, *any* other set, might work? My mother and father are happy for a time. Truly. My mother has found a man who can teach her Arabic and deepen her understanding of Islam.

A devout man. A loving and spontaneous man. A man who loved my sister at first sight—who got down on the floor to play with her the moment they met. My father is striking and painfully thin because he's been living in a boardinghouse where he's not allowed to cook. His English is already near perfect, if a bit stately. He has a touch of an Arabic accent. Occasionally, he misspeaks, but the effect is usually comical. He loves spaghetti and meatballs, but refers to it as "spaghetti and balls meat." My mother can't help but laugh at this. He isn't offended. "You are my heart," he tells her. "It is right that you should correct me."

By July, my father has found his new family an apartment in the Oakland section of Pittsburgh. My mother feels buoyant for the first time in years. The neighborhood is bustling with culture and full of students like her. Rihan and Omar live close by. The *masjid* is just a couple of blocks away. My mother and father go shopping arm in arm for food and decorations for the apartment. She asks him what kinds of things he likes. "I like everything you like," he tells her. "You are the queen of our home, and I want you to arrange everything as you like. If you are happy with everything you pick, I will love it, too."

I am born in March 1983, and my brother a year later. When I'm three, Baba takes me to the Kennywood Amusement Park. On the Dizzy Dynamo, we spin around in giant cups. And on the Grand Carousel, we ride the painted horses: my father chooses a gold stallion that glides up and down, while I cling to the neck of a stationary brown pony. Later in the day, on a miniature roller coaster called Lil' Phantom, my father pretends to be terrified—"O Allah, protect me and deliver me to my destination!"—to distract me from the fact that *I* actually *am* terrified. I will always remember this day. It is my earliest memory. Not even the coming nightmares will blot it out.

• • •

My father does not harden against America overnight. His bitterness builds slowly, coaxed along by random encounters with ugliness and misfortune. At the mosque, my mother starts helping Rihan with *da'wa*—the campaign to bring new converts to the faith. They don't go door to door or proselytize on the street; they meet with visitors at the *masjid*, educate them about Islam, and answer the sort of questions that my mother herself once had. Many of the visitors are young American women. Girls, really. Some come to the mosque not because they're on a spiritual journey but because they've fallen in love with a Muslim man. Still, enough genuinely curious seekers come through the doors of the mosque—and ultimately convert—to make my mother's work with Rihan fulfilling. Sometimes, if the women have nowhere to stay, my family offers them a bed.

Which turns out to be a mistake. In the fall of 1985, my family welcomes a young woman named Barbara into our home. (I've changed her name, since she's not here to offer her own version of what follows.) Barbara is sullen and erratic, and looks no one in the eyes. She stays with us for months. Barbara doesn't seem to be truly interested in Islam. Her sister is checking out the religion to make her boyfriend happy, and Barbara is just tagging along. She radiates such an uncomfortable energy that it's hard even to sit in the same room with her.

Soon, she is hanging around with what my parents warn her is "a really bad crowd of Muslims" from another neighborhood. My mother tries to marry Barbara off twice, and twice Barbara is rejected after a single meeting. Her self-esteem plummets. She starts sitting in the tub, fully clothed, and crying in the middle of the night. She accuses us, all of us, of stealing her clothes from her room—clothes no Muslim could wear, let alone a child. My father insists that she move out. She does. Less than a week later—apparently acting on advice from her new Muslim friends, who think she might be able to make some money off my family—she accuses my father of raping her.

There is a rapist loose in Pittsburgh at the moment. Some of his victims have described him as "either Hispanic or Middle Eastern." The police take Barbara's allegation with the utmost seriousness. By the time a lawyer friend of my family convinces them that the woman has invented the story, my father has been flattened by fear and humiliation. He has stopped getting into bed with my mother at night. He's parked his prayer rug by the radiator in the living room, and curled into a ball on top of it. He has stopped eating. All he does is sleep and pray for his safety. Even the members of the mosque don't know who to believe—they seem to be split down the middle, as far as my mother can tell—which intensifies my father's pain until it's like a tumor growing in his stomach. A hearing is held at the *masjid*. The mosque's board members are alarmed by the dissent in their midst, and want to settle the matter themselves. They do not trust the American justice system anyway.

My mother will describe the scene at the mosque for me many years later: Barbara arrives with her sister, her sister's boyfriend, and a volatile crowd of Muslim friends. The tension is prickly enough that a fight breaks out. My father sits silently, his head lowered, his hands clutching his knees. Barbara repeats her accusations— my father raped her and my family stole her clothes—and demands restitution. My mother's heart breaks for her husband. To have his devotion to Allah questioned in his own mosque!

A board member asks Barbara to describe my father's body.

"Hairy," she says. "Hairy chest. Hairy back. *Hairy*."

My mother barks out a laugh.

My father springs to his feet. He addresses the board: "Would you like me to take my shirt off *right now* so you can see what a liar this woman is?" As fate would have it, his body does not conform to the Middle Eastern stereotype.

My father is told it will not be necessary for him

to disrobe. The board members are convinced of his innocence. To settle the matter, they give Barbara $150 for the clothes she insists were taken. She seems pleased. She and her retinue sweep out of the mosque. As if her lack of respect for Islam wasn't clear enough, she has worn her shoes inside the mosque the entire time.

● ● ●

My parents try to rebuild their lives in Pittsburgh, but the pieces won't go back together. For my father, the mortification has been too great. Sadness and exhaustion hang in the air. My mother is too frightened to do outreach anymore. My father cannot face his friends from the *masjid*. Or anyone else, really. He works. He grows thinner. My only memory of him from this time is of him kneeling on his prayer rug in the living room, doubled over in prayer or pain or both.

4 1986
Jersey City, New Jersey

In July, we move away from Pittsburgh, and—for a while—our lives are filled with light again. My mother teaches first grade at an Islamic school in Jersey City. My father can no longer find work as a jeweler, but he gets a job at a company that installs stage lighting, and becomes pleasantly pudgy from my mother's cooking. They grow closer and closer. The Egyptian community in the city is a marvel: there are Arabic stores everywhere, and men in tunics and women in *hijab* flow through the streets en masse. Our new mosque, Masjid Al-Shams, doesn't have all the activities for women and families that my mother is used to, but we go regularly for prayers. (I've changed the name of the mosque out of respect for its current congregation.) After work, my father picnics with us in the park. He plays baseball and soccer with me in the yard—or a preschool version of it, anyway. A true calm descends on the family. And then one day the principal of the school where my mom teaches calls her into his office, and tells her that everything's okay, not to worry, it's going to be fine, but he's just received a call: My father has been in an accident at work. He's at St. Vincent's Hospital in New York.

Baba's been electrocuted. He'll recover, but the shock

was sufficient to burn his hand, which was holding a screwdriver, throw him off a ladder, and knock him unconscious. He undergoes surgery. The dead skin is laboriously peeled away, and skin from his thigh grafted on to his hand. My father is taught how to care for his burns, and sent back home to recover with pain meds, as well as a prescription for an unpredictable, heavy-duty antidepressant. He cannot work. Being able to support his family has always been critical to him as a man and as a Muslim.

Though the family can get by on my mother's salary and food stamps, shame spreads through his body like a drop of red dye in water. My mother sees that he's suffering, but Baba is beyond her reach. In many ways, his behavior mirrors the way he acted during the rape allegation. This time, though, my father just doesn't pray obsessively, he pores endlessly over the Qur'an. Even when he can work again—he gets the job maintaining the heat and air-conditioning at the courthouse in Manhattan—he is more inward than ever. He goes to Masjid Al-Shams constantly, praying, listening to lectures, and going to mysterious meetings. The mosque initially seemed moderate, but it has grown into one of the most fundamentalist in the city—which explains why my mother doesn't feel particularly welcome there as a woman, and why there's an anger in the air there that we've never experienced before. It also explains why my father is growing palpably less tolerant of non-Muslims. My mother brings my sister, my brother, and

me to family activities at the Islamic Center above my
sister's school, but Baba will not come with us: suddenly,
he doesn't approve of the imam there. At home, he
still has moments of warmth with us kids, but there's
an increasing number of times when he looks *through*
us, not *at* us—when he's just a figure brushing by us,
clutching a Qur'an. One day, I innocently ask when he
became such a devout Muslim, and he tells me, with a
new edge in his voice, "When I came to this country and
saw everything that was wrong with it."

Many years later, FBI agents would reportedly give
Masjid Al-Shams a chilling nickname: "the Jersey jihad
office."

• • •

By the late eighties, the eyes of Muslims everywhere
are on Afghanistan. The Soviet Union and the United
States have been using the country as a Cold War game
board for almost a decade. In 1979, the communist
Afghan government requested Russian troops to help
fight the mujahedeen rebels (a resistance comprised of
various loosely aligned Afghan opposition groups). In
response, an alliance led by the United States and Saudi
Arabia began funneling billions of dollars in money
and weapons to the rebels themselves. The violence has
been such that a third of the Afghan population has fled,
mostly to Pakistan.

My father's mosque is just a peeling gray smudge on
the third floor of a storefront, its downstairs neighbors

a Chinese takeout restaurant and a jewelry store. Still, Masjid Al-Shams attracts sheikhs and scholars from around the world who exhort Baba and his friends to come to the aid of their rebel brothers. For my father and other struggling, disenfranchised members of the mosque, the sense of purpose is intoxicating. One of the speakers in particular entrances my father: a Sunni firebrand from Palestine named Abdullah Yusuf Azzam.

Azzam's on a fund-raising tour of the States, rallying audiences with a stark battle cry: "Jihad and the rifle alone: no negotiations, no conferences, and no dialogues." He has already mentored a young economics student from Saudi Arabia, Osama bin Laden, and persuaded him to bring his family's connections (and his family's checkbook) to Pakistan to support the fight against the Russians. "We will continue the jihad no matter how long the way," Azzam promises the American Muslims who flock to his talks, "until the last breath and the last beat of the pulse." He inspires them with tales from the battlefield that veer into magical realism—stories of mujahedeen whose bodies are impervious to Soviet bullets, who are accompanied in combat by angels on horseback, and who are protected from falling bombs by squadrons of birds.

My father meets Azzam at the mosque and returns home transformed. His whole life the world has acted upon *him*; here, at long last, is *his* chance to act—and make a clear and irrefutable demonstration of his devotion to Allah. He and men from the mosque start meeting in our apartment, talking loudly, ecstatically, about supporting the jihad in Afghanistan. They set up a shop on the floor below the *masjid*, where they sell religious texts, posters, and cassettes to raise money. It's a dim, windowless space. There are books everywhere. The walls are covered with teachings from the Qur'an, written in giant, swooping glitter. Baba takes my brother and me there all the time, and we help out. We have no real idea what is going on, but there's no mistaking that my father is *alive* again.

My mother approves of the Afghan jihad—to a degree. She is both a devout Muslim and a patriotic American, and while these identities are often at odds, the alliance between the Muslim rebels and the Americans in Afghanistan is a rare instance in which her religious and political leaders agree on something. But my father is hurtling forward too fast. He now has a direct line to Azzam, whom he idolizes. He and the men from the mosque go on camping trips to practice survival skills. They drive out to the Calverton Shooting Range on Long Island for target practice. When the head of the mosque expresses concern over its radicalization, they push him out of his post. It probably goes without saying that my father no longer has any time for my mother and us kids, but there it is. When he tags along for my first day at a new school, my mother is shocked. Not long ago, his family was his abiding concern; now we are competing for his attention with Muslims around the globe.

The breaking point comes when my father tells my

mother that he no longer wants to support the jihad from afar: He wants to go to Afghanistan and take up arms. My mother is terrified. She begs him to reconsider. He will not. And there's more: He insists that my mother move to Egypt with us kids to live with my grandfather while he joins the mujahedeen. Fortunately, my grandfather is appalled by the plan. He believes that my father's place is with his wife and children, and he rejects the proposal. He goes so far as to tell my father that, if indeed we move to Egypt, he will disown us and watch us starve.

My father doesn't have long to mourn the death of his dreams. In 1989, someone (it will never be clear who) attempts to assassinate Azzam by packing his pulpit in Peshawar, Pakistan, with explosives. The bomb does not go off. On November twenty-fourth of that same year, however, Azzam and his two sons are in a Jeep on the way to Friday prayers when an assassin detonates a bomb under the road. All three are killed. It is difficult to convey the effect of the news on my father. Looking back over two decades later, my mother will pinpoint Azzam's murder as the moment she lost her husband forever.

In 1989, the Soviets give up on Afghanistan and withdraw. The United States, with nothing at stake in the region anymore, decamps as well. Afghanistan has become a nation of widows and orphans, its people, economy, and infrastructure ravaged. Jihadists such as my father long to create the first true Muslim state in the world—a country run by Islamic law, known as

sharia. In 1990, one of Osama bin Laden's allies, the
blind Egyptian sheikh Omar Abdel-Rahman, travels to
America to rally the faithful for a truly global jihad that
not only reclaims Afghanistan but also puts an end, by
any means necessary, to what they see as the American-
sponsored tyranny of Israel over Palestine. The Blind
Sheikh is on the State Department's terrorist watch list,
and rightfully so: He's been imprisoned in the Middle
East for issuing the fatwa that led to the assassination
of Egyptian president Anwar Sadat. Rahman manages
to wrangle a tourist visa nonetheless. When the State
Department revokes it, he convinces the Immigration
and Naturalization Service office in New Jersey to give
him a green card. Government agencies, it seems, cannot
agree on how to handle an international terrorist who
was just our ally against the Russians.

Around this time, we move from Jersey City to
Cliffside Park at my mother's insistence. It's a quiet,
leafy suburb—it's just gotten its close-up as Tom Hanks's
hometown in *Big*—and my mother hopes that distance
will break the bond between my father and the radicals
at Masjid Al-Shams. In truth, it changes nothing.
Every morning he rails at her, quoting passages from
the Qur'an and from Muhammad's teachings in the
Hadith. Islam says *this*, wife, Islam says *that*. My father
has become a stranger to her. Every night after work,
he makes the long drive back to our old mosque or to a
new one, in Brooklyn, where the Blind Sheikh is also
captivating the faithful. My father's obsession with

the plight of Muslims in Palestine deepens, as does his disgust for America's support of Israel. He's not alone in this, of course. My whole life—in mosques, in living rooms, at fund-raisers for Hamas—I've been told that Israel is the enemy of Islam. But the words sound harder now. My mother worries that some sort of disaster is headed our way. She goes on what she'll later call "autopilot," devoting herself to us kids and just trying to get through the dark tunnel of days.

My father brings me to hear the Blind Sheikh speak many times. I don't understand enough Arabic to grasp more than a few scattered words, but his ferocity frightens me. When my father ushers me up to shake Rahman's hand after the sermon, I just nod shyly. Then they put plastic sheeting down on the floor of the mosque and the men bring *fatteh*—toasted pita and rice covered with lamb soup—out for dinner. For an hour, the voices of parents and children are like birds in the air, and everything seems warm and ordinary again and we eat.

My father grows closer to the Blind Sheikh. Unbeknownst to us, the sheikh is apparently urging him to make a name for himself in the movement. My father considers assassinating the future prime minister of Israel, Ariel Sharon, and goes so far as to stake out his hotel. He eventually gives up on the plan, but for a fundamentalist who believes himself to be a living instrument of Allah's righteous fury, potential targets are everywhere. Soon, my father discovers what he believes to be his true calling: he must murder Rabbi Kahane.

• • •

Here is one of the last memories I have of my father as
a free man: It's a Saturday morning in Jersey City. Late
summer. Baba wakes my brother and me up early—we've
fallen back asleep after praying before sunrise—and tells
us to prepare for an adventure. We dress and follow him
drowsily out to the car. We drive and drive and drive: out
of our green suburb, across the tense, congested Bronx,
and onto Long Island. Two hours go by, which feel like
four to my brother and me. Finally, we arrive at a big blue
sign: CALVERTON SHOOTING RANGE.

We pull into a sandy lot, and I see that Ammu
Ibrahim is waiting for us, along with another car, full
of my father's friends. My uncle is leaning back against
his sedan while his boys run around happily, kicking
up sand. He's wearing a T-shirt that bears a map of
Afghanistan and a slogan: HELP EACH OTHER IN GOODNESS
AND PIETY. The men all wish one another peace, then one
of my father's friends pops open the trunk of his car,
which is full of pistols and AK-47s.

The targets—silhouettes of faceless men—stand in
front of steep embankments. There's a flashing yellow
light on top of each of them, and a ring of fir trees atop
the hills beyond. Every so often a rabbit will scurry out,
get spooked by the crackle of gunfire, and scurry back in.

Baba and Ammu shoot first, then us kids. We take
turns for a while. I had no idea my father had become

such a marksman. As for me, the rifle is heavy in my arms, and I don't have nearly as good aim as my cousins, who tease me every time I miss the target and hit the embankment, the bullet sending up a tiny spray of sand.

A low ceiling of clouds slides over the shooting range, casting everything in shadow. A half-hearted rain starts to fall. We're about to pack it in when, on my final turn, something strange happens: I accidentally shoot out the light on top of the target, and it shatters—explodes, really—and sets the silhouette of the man on fire.

I turn to Baba, my whole body clenched, worrying that I've done something wrong.

Strangely, he grins and nods approvingly.

Next to him, Ammu laughs. He and my father are close. He must know that my father is planning to kill Kahane. "*Ibn abu,*" he says, with a broad smile.

The implication of Ammu's words will trouble me for years, until I realize that my uncle is entirely wrong about me.

"*Ibn abu.*"

Like father, like son.

5 January 1991
Rikers Island Correctional Facility, New York

We wait forever for the van. We're in this immense parking lot—the biggest parking lot I've ever seen—and the world is gray and cold, and there's nothing to do, nothing to look at, nothing but a silver lunch truck surrounded by fog. My mother gives us kids five dollars, and we wander over to check it out. The truck is selling knishes, among other things. I've never heard of a knish—it sounds like something Dr. Seuss invented—but the spelling is so cool and weird that I buy one. It turns out to be a deep-fried something-or-other filled with potato. When I'm older, I'll discover that knishes are Jewish pastries, and I will remember having slathered one with mustard and devoured it on the way to Rikers Island, where my father was awaiting trial for shooting one of the world's most prominent, and divisive, rabbis in the neck.

When we arrive at Rikers, we join a long, snaking, boisterous line of visitors, most of them women and children. I can see how much it pains my mother to have to bring her children here. She keeps us pressed close. She has told us that Baba has been accused of killing a Jewish rabbi, but is quick to add that only Baba himself can tell us if that's true.

We're funneled through security. The checkpoints
seem to be endless. At one of them, a guard puts on
a rubber glove and fishes around inside my mother's
mouth. At another, we're all searched and patted
down—a simple matter for my brother and me but a
complicated one for Islamic women and girls wearing
hijab that they're forbidden from taking off in public.
My mother and sister are whisked off to private rooms
by female officers. For half an hour, my brother and I sit
alone, swinging our legs and doing a bad job of looking
brave. Finally, we're all reunited and ushered down
a concrete hallway toward the visiting room. Then
suddenly, for the first time in months, Baba is right in
front of us.

He's wearing an orange jumpsuit. He has a badly
bloodshot eye. My father, now thirty-six, seems
haggard, exhausted, and not entirely like himself. At
the sight of us, though, his eyes get bright with love. We
run to him.

After a melee of hugs and kisses—after he's bound
the four of us up in his arms like one giant bundle—my
father assures us that he is innocent. He wanted to talk
to Kahane, to tell him about Islam, to convince him that
Muslims were not his enemies. He promises us that he
did not have a gun, and that he is not a murderer. Even
before he's finished speaking, my mother is sobbing.
"I *knew* it," she says. "In my heart, I knew it, I knew it, I
knew it."

My father talks to my sister, my brother, and me one by

one. He asks us the same two questions he will ask us for years whenever he sees us or writes to us: *Are you making your prayers? Are you being good to your mother?*

"We are still a family, Z," he tells me. "And I am still your father. No matter where I am. No matter what people may say about me. Do you understand?"

"Yes, Baba."

"Yet you are not looking at me, Z. Let me see those eyes I gave you, please."

"Yes, Baba."

"Ah, but *my* eyes are green! Your eyes—they are green, then blue, then purple. You must decide what color your eyes are, Z!"

"I will, Baba."

"Very good. Now play with your brother and sister because"—here my father turns to my mother, and smiles at her warmly—"I must talk to my queen."

I flop onto the floor, and pull a few games from my backpack: Connect Four and Chutes and Ladders. My mother and father sit at the table, holding hands firmly and talking in low tones they think we can't hear. My mother is pretending to be stronger than she is. She's telling him she's fine, she can handle the kids in his absence; she's only worried about him. She has been holding her questions in so long that they all come out in a rush: *Are you safe, Sayyid? Are you getting enough to eat? Are there other Muslims here? Do the guards let you pray? What can I bring you? What can I tell you, Sayyid, besides I love you, I love you, I love you?*

• • •

We haven't returned to our apartment in Cliffside Park since the shooting, just as my mother feared we wouldn't when she laid the white sheet on my floor and told me to fill it. We're living at Uncle Ibrahim's place in Brooklyn temporarily—three adults and six children in a one-bedroom apartment—and trying to build a new normal, brick by brick.

The New York police raided our home just hours after we left it. It will be years before I'm old enough to read the details, and by then I'll know that my father was lying when he told us he was not a murderer. The police carted away forty-seven boxes of suspicious materials suggesting an international conspiracy—bomb-making instructions, a hit list of potential Jewish targets, and references to an attack on "the world's high buildings." But most of the material is in Arabic, and authorities dismiss some of the notes as "Islamic poetry." No one will bother translating the bulk of it until after the first World Trade Center attack less than three years later. (Around the same time, federal agents will arrest my Uncle Ibrahim and, while searching his apartment, find fake Nicaraguan passports in my family's names. If my father's plan to kill Kahane had gone off without a hitch, I'd apparently have grown up in Central America with a Spanish name.) The authorities aren't just ignoring the forty-seven boxes from our apartment. The FBI also has surveillance footage of my father and others training at the Calverton Shooting Range—but nobody has connected the dots. The NYPD chief of detectives insists that my father was a lone gunman. The idea is absurd, as the investigative journalist Peter Lance and the U.S. government itself will prove long after the fact.

For years, theories will flourish that my father entered the Marriott with at least one, possibly two, other conspirators, though no one else will ever be charged. My father was wearing a yarmulke to blend in with the mostly Orthodox crowd. He approached the podium, where Kahane was declaiming with his signature fury about the Arab menace. My father paused, and then said aloud, "This is the moment!" Then he fired at the rabbi, and raced out of the ballroom. One of Kahane's supporters, a seventy-three-year-old, tried to block him. My father shot the man in the leg, then continued out onto the street. According to reports, his friend Red, the taxi driver who would call my mother that night, was supposed to be waiting outside the Marriott in his cab. A doorman, however, had apparently told him to move along. So my father got into the wrong cab. After the cab had gone one block, another of Kahane's supporters stepped in front of it to stop my father from getting away. My father put his gun to the driver's head. The driver leaped out of the cab. Then my father leaped out, too. He ran down Lexington, exchanged fire with the postal

officer, who was wearing a bulletproof vest, and fell
to the street. According to some theories, my father's
accomplices escaped via the subway.

History will prove that my father did not act alone. But
it's 1990, and the NYPD can't yet fathom the concept of a
global terror cell—virtually no one can—and they have no
interest in trying to prosecute one.

• • •

We haven't returned to our old school in Cliffside Park,
either. The media descended on it the morning after the
assassination, and we no longer felt safe or welcome there.
Knowing we have nowhere to go, Al-Ghazaly, the Islamic
school in Jersey City, has offered us all scholarships. It
turns out that the slogan on Ammu Ibrahim's T-shirt—
HELP EACH OTHER IN GOODNESS AND PIETY—can be a call to
kindness, not just violence.

My mother gratefully accepts the scholarships and
moves us back to Jersey City. All we can afford is a place
on a derelict stretch of Reservoir Avenue. My mother
asks the landlord to install bars on the windows, but
that doesn't stop drunks from harassing my sister, my
brother, and me when we play in the street. We move
again, this time to an equally sketchy spot on Saint Paul
Avenue. One day, when my mother leaves to pick us up
at school, someone breaks in, steals whatever he can
carry, and leaves a knife on our computer keyboard. In
the midst of all this, we return to school. I'm in the first
grade. It's the middle of the year, the worst possible

time to transfer, even if I *weren't* a shy kid and my family *wasn't* infamous.

My first morning at Al-Ghazaly, I warily approach the doors to the classroom. They're arched and enormous—it's like I'm walking into the mouth of a whale. The room is abuzz with activity. The minute I step inside, though, all heads turn. Everything stops dead. There's silence for two seconds. *One* Mississippi, *two* Mississippi. And then the kids are leaping to their feet. They're pushing back their chairs, which screech against the floor, and they're rushing toward me. It happens so fast that I can't decipher the energy. Is it hostile? Euphoric? Have I done something unforgivable, or hit a game-winning homerun? The kids are shouting now, one louder than the next. They're all asking the same question: *Did your father kill Rabbi Kahane?* It seems like they want me to say yes, and that I'll disappoint them if I say no. The teacher is trying to get to me. She's peeling the kids away, telling them to sit down, sit down, sit down. In my awkwardness, all I can think to do—more than two decades later I still wince at the memory—is shrug my shoulders and smile.

• • •

In those first wintry months of 1991, the media and much of the world believe Baba to be a monster, and my mother hears rumors that the Jewish Defense League has declared a sort of fatwa of its own: "Kill the sons of Nosair." Yet to many Muslims my father is a hero and a

martyr. Kahane, the argument goes, was himself a bigot,
a proponent of violence and vengeance, an extremist
condemned even by many of his own faith. He referred
to Arabs as dogs. He wanted Israel swept clean of them—
by force if necessary. So while my father is demonized
in many quarters, Muslim families thank us on the
street and send donations from all over the world. The
donations make it possible for my family to eat—and
for me and my siblings to have the only extravagances
of our childhoods. One night, my mother presents us
with a Sears catalogue and tells us we can have anything
we want. I pick every piece of Teenage Mutant Ninja
Turtle merchandise I can find. Then, at Al-Ghazaly, I
discover that one of my classmates' fathers is so elated by
Kahane's murder that he'll stop me every time he sees me
and hand me a hundred-dollar bill. I try to run into him
as much as possible. I buy my first Game Boy with his
money. The world may be sending me mixed messages,
but a Game Boy is a Game Boy.

   An activist-lawyer named Michael Tarif Warren
has been representing my father. When the legendary
civil rights advocate and unabashed radical William
Kunstler unexpectedly offers his services as well,
Warren graciously accepts the help. Kunstler has a long,
mournful face, glasses perched above his forehead, and
wild gray hair. He is lively and warm with us, and he
believes in my father's right to a fair trial. Sometimes,
Kunstler and his team camp out in our apartment and
strategize with my mother until all hours. Other times,

we visit him in his office in Greenwich Village. He has a statue of Michelangelo's *David* on his desk. Whenever we stop by, out of respect for my sister and mother, he takes off his tie and drapes it around the little guy's neck to cover his private parts.

Kunstler hopes to convince the jury that Kahane's own people murdered him in an argument over money, then framed my father. My mother believes the story herself— her husband has assured her that he's innocent, and there must be *some* explanation for the assassination— and we all get swept up in my father's cause. $163,000 is reportedly donated for Baba's defense. Ammu Ibrahim reaches out to Osama bin Laden, who contributes twenty thousand himself.

We visit my father at Rikers again and again. I see him in a prison uniform so many times that it will color my previous memories of him. Over two decades later, I will picture my family around the dinner table in Cliffside Park, a year or more before my father's arrest. I'll imagine him talking to us cheerfully, passing a platter of lamb—and wearing an orange jumpsuit.

6 December 21, 1991
New York Supreme Court, Manhattan

My father's supporters sit on one side of the courtroom, Kahane's on the other, like at a wedding. The factions have broken out into fights on the sidewalk during the trial, so there are thirty-five police officers in court today. It's a Saturday. The jury has been deliberating for four days. They've heard the state argue that El-Sayyid Nosair was a hate-fueled man, acting alone. They've seen the lead prosecutor hold up the .357 Magnum, stare at my father, and then turn to them and say, "This gun took one life, wounded two others, and scared an awful lot of people. Tell them by your verdict: not here, Nosair, not here."

Jurors have also heard Kunstler's team contend that Kahane was murdered by enemies within his own entourage, and that the killers framed my father by placing the murder weapon next to him as he lay bleeding on Lexington Avenue. They've been reminded repeatedly that, thanks to the mayhem at the Marriott, not one witness remembers seeing my father shoot Kahane.

By the time the jury returns with their verdict, it's late in the afternoon and we're at home in Jersey City. The phone rings. My mother answers. It's Uncle Ibrahim's wife, Amina. She's shouting so loud that even I can hear her: "He's not guilty! He's not guilty!"

The courtroom erupts after the verdict. There are screams of fury from one side and cries of relief from the other. They're like two opposing storm fronts. As for the judge, he is appalled by the jury's verdict. He tells them it's "devoid of common sense and logic." Then, as if he fears he hasn't made himself clear, he adds, "I believe the defendant conducted a rape of this country, of our Constitution and of our laws, and of people seeking to exist peacefully together."

The jury *has* found my father guilty of lesser charges: criminal possession of a weapon, assault (of the postal officer and the elderly man) and coercion (in the hijacking of the taxi). The judge sentences him to the maximum sentence permissible by law, seven to twenty-two years. But the courtroom is still roiling, even as the jurors file out. One of Kahane's followers points to the empty jury box and shouts, "That was no jury of our peers!" Still more are chanting, "Death to Nosair! Death to Nosair! Arab dogs will die!"

• • •

The fact that my father's been found not guilty of murder gives my family just enough hope to end up hurting us. His lawyers vow to appeal the convictions. I'm eight years old now, and I am convinced that Baba will be walking through the door at any moment, and that we will be resuming our lives. But my father never shows up. And every day he *doesn't,* I withdraw deeper.

Within a year of the trial, donations to my family slow to a trickle and become difficult to live on. My father's friends are still loyal to us (a deliveryman named Mohammed Salameh promises to marry my sister when she comes of age) but they're more loyal to the jihad (Salameh will be sentenced to 240 years in prison for his part in the World Trade Center attack before my sister even enters her teens). We move around New Jersey and Pennsylvania constantly, usually because there's been a death threat. By the time I finish high school, I'll have moved twenty times.

We always live in dangerous neighborhoods, without another Muslim family in sight. I get punched and kicked at school because I'm different, because I'm pudgy and don't talk much. My mother gets taunted on the street— called a *ghost* and a *ninja*—because of her headscarf and veil. And there is no permanence to anything. Someone always discovers who we are. The word spreads that we are *those* Nosairs. The fear and humiliation return, and we move again.

Amidst all this, there is the nonstop emptiness of *missing my dad*. His absence gets bigger and bigger until there's no room in my brain for anything else. He's not there to play soccer with me. He's not there to tell me how to handle bullies. He's not there to protect my mother from the people in the street. He's in Attica State Prison— and won't be out until I'm at least fifteen, maybe not even until I'm twenty-nine. (I do the math in my head all the time.) I tell myself that I can't count on him anymore. But whenever we visit him, hope returns. Seeing the family together again makes everything seem possible, even when it isn't.

• • •

One weekend when I'm nine, my mother drives us across New York to Attica, which is on the far edge of the state, near Canada. The car's an old station wagon with fake wood paneling on the sides. My mother has folded the back seats down so we can sleep or play or roll around if we want to. Ever since we left New Jersey, I've been bubbling over with nervous energy. This weekend we're not just going to visit my father in some big, boring room where there's nothing to do but play Chinese checkers. This weekend we're going to "live" with my father. My mother has tried to explain how that's possible, but I still can't picture it. We stop for groceries along the way—somehow or other, she's going to cook for us all—and my mother lets me buy a box of Entenmann's chocolate chip cookies. The soft kind. When we get back in the car, I'm twice as excited as I was before, thrilled about seeing Baba *and* about the cookies. My mother looks at me in the rearview mirror and laughs. She never gets to see me happy anymore.

Attica is massive and gray—it's like the castle of a depressed king. We go through security. The guards inspect everything, even the groceries, which have to be perfectly sealed.

"We got a problem here," one of them says.

He is holding up the Entenmann's. There's something wrong with the box. It turns out that there's a hole in the cellophane window on top, so they won't let me take it in. My eyes start stinging with tears. I know that the minute we walk away, the guards are going to eat my cookies. They *know* there's nothing wrong with them.

My mother puts a hand on my shoulder. "Guess what," she whispers.

If I answer, my voice will break, and I don't want to embarrass myself in front of the guards, so I just look at my mother expectantly until she leans down and says these amazing words in my ear: "I bought another box."

I run across the grass toward my father. He's grinning broadly and waving for me to run faster, faster, faster. He's standing in front of a white, suburban, one-story house that's been plunked down inside Attica's walls so families like ours can spend the weekend together. There's a picnic table, a swing set, an outdoor grill. I'm out of breath when I reach my father. I throw my arms around his waist, and he reaches down to pick me up. He pretends I've gotten too big for him to lift—"Ya Allah," he groans, "Z must be short for Z-normous!"—and he falls on his back in the newly cut grass. We wrestle for a few moments, then my brother calls from the swing set, "Push me, Baba, push me!"

The weekend is perfect—even the boring moments are perfect, because they're *normal*. We play soccer with the family from the house next door. We have spaghetti and meatballs for dinner, and a plate of Entenmann's for dessert. Then my parents say goodnight early and disappear into a bedroom. My sister tells our little brother he should go to bed but he says he's not tired, not even the tiniest bit—then falls asleep within thirty seconds on a black leather couch in the living room. So my sister and I seize the moment and watch a videotape of *Cujo*, which I snuck into our basket at the prison library. It's about this sweet Saint Bernard that gets bitten by a bat and gets rabies, then starts going mental in Connecticut. My sister and I snuggle close as we watch. Our mother would go mental herself if she knew we were watching it, which adds to the thrill.

So for one weekend we actually *are* the family that Baba insists we will always be. Yes, the phone rings each night at six PM, and my father has to recite his full name and his prison identification number and some other stuff to prove that he hasn't tried to escape. Yes, there's a fence topped with barbed wire running along the perimeter of our green suburban yard. And yes, beyond that, there's a colossal, gray thirty-foot wall. But the five of us are together, and the world doesn't seem like a threat. It's as if the big gray wall is protecting us—keeping other people *out*, rather than my father *in*.

As always, there's more to the picture than I understand. Baba may be a gentle Saint Bernard when he's with us, but the moment we leave he turns rabid again. When we pile back into the station wagon for the endless drive back to New Jersey—dazed and happy and full of all that dangerous hope—my father returns to his cell and rants about the Jewish judge who sentenced him to prison and instructs visitors from the mosque to murder him ("Why should I be merciful with him? Was he merciful with me?"). When that plan fails, he turns his attention to an even more vile plot. While I am fantasizing about being a real family, he is fantasizing about bringing down the Twin Towers.

7 February 26, 1993
Jersey City, New Jersey

I'm about to turn ten, and I've been bullied at school for years. I can't pretend it's just because of who my father is. For reasons I will probably spend my whole life trying to unravel, I seem to be a magnet for abuse. The bullies' latest trick is to wait until I've turned to open my locker and then slam my head against it and run. Whenever this happens, the principal says he wants to be "fair to all parties," so I usually get sent to detention along with the bullies. The anger and dread have made a permanent nest in my stomach. Today's a Friday, and my mother has let me stay home from school to recover from what we agree to call "a stomach bug."

I'm camped out on the couch, watching *Harry and the Hendersons*, a movie about a family who's hiding a Bigfoot-type creature from the police because the police won't understand how kind and gentle he is. In the middle of the movie, there's breaking news. My mother's in her bedroom, trying to write a historical novel, so she's not there to turn off the TV this time.

There's been an explosion in the parking lot beneath the North Tower of the World Trade Center. The NYPD, the FBI, and the ATF are on the scene, the early theory being that a transformer has exploded.

I knock on my mother's bedroom door. When she doesn't answer, I crack open the door a bit. My mother is sitting at her desk. She's engrossed in writing her novel—it's about an American woman who goes to the Middle East and has some kind of adventure, that's all I know—and she's typing in a sort of trance.

"You should come out," I say. "There's something going on."

"Can't," she says, without looking up.

"But—"

"Stop it, Z. My heroine's caught in a sandstorm, and her camel won't budge."

So I flop back on the couch and watch the story unfold for hours. The wreckage is horrific. People are stumbling out covered in ash. The reporter is saying, "We've never seen anything like this before." At three PM, my mother comes out of her bedroom, blinking in the sunlight like she's emerging from a cave. She looks at the TV and stops short.

"Why didn't you *tell* me?" she says.

• • •

Hundreds of FBI agents comb through the rubble at the blast site. They abandon the theory about the transformer when they discover remnants of the Ryder van that carried the explosives. The FBI traces the van back to Mohammed Salameh—the deliveryman who'd promised to marry my sister when she came of age—and arrests him on March fourth when he returns to the

rental company to report the van stolen and demand
that he get his four-hundred-dollar deposit back. In the
months that follow, America shivers at the previously
incomprehensible thought of terrorism at home, as
well as at the fact that its governmental agencies had
been caught unawares. It will be years before the last
conspirator is convicted, but alarming details surface
daily about how the plot came together.

A startling fact emerges: My father helped strategize
the attack from his cell at Attica, using visitors as
go-betweens to associates back home. One of those
associates was his old mentor, the Blind Sheikh, who
was still residing—and issuing fatwas—in the States,
despite being a known terrorist. The Blind Sheikh offered
his followers "spiritual guidance." He encouraged
not just the WTC plot, according to the government,
but also signed off on a plan that would have been far
more deadly, had it ever come to pass: five more bombs
detonated within ten minutes at the United Nations, the
Lincoln and Holland Tunnels, the George Washington
Bridge, and a federal building housing the FBI in New
York City.

For practical purposes, though, the WTC operation
was run by the Kuwaiti-born Ramzi Yousef. He had
studied electrical engineering in Wales and bomb-
making at a terrorist training camp in Pakistan. He
entered the United States with a fake Iraqi passport in
1992 and, upon being detained, played a get-out-of-jail-
free card by requesting asylum. A court date was set.

And, because holding cells were full, Yousef was released on his own recognizance in New Jersey, whereupon he and his team began collecting the ingredients for the bomb. Just hours after the attack, Yousef left the country, without inconvenience. "We declare our responsibility for the explosion on the mentioned building," he said in a letter to the *New York Times*. "This action was done in response for the American political, economical, and military support to Israel, the state of terrorism, and to the rest of the dictator countries in the region."

The six victims, of course, had no ties whatsoever to American foreign policy. In truth, the bombing was an act of hatred destined—like all such acts— only to inspire more hatred in its turn. I wish I could do more to honor the innocents than just repeat their names, but I'd be ashamed if I didn't do at least that much. All of them died simply living their lives: Robert Kirkpatrick, Bill Macko, and Stephen Knapp were all maintenance supervisors at the WTC. They were eating lunch together when the bomb went off. Monica Rodriguez Smith was a secretary. She was seven months pregnant and doing clerical work when she was killed. Wilfredo Mercado worked for the restaurant Windows on the World. He was checking in deliveries. And John DiGiovanni was a salesman who specialized in dental products—he was just parking his car.

By the fall of 1995, the government has gotten around to translating the full contents of the forty-seven boxes taken from our home after Kahane's assassination.

They have determined that the killing was indeed part of a conspiracy, and—thanks to some double-jeopardy loophole—retried my father for the murder, as well as for his part in the World Trade Center bombing.

My father still insists that he is innocent of absolutely everything. I believe him because—well, because I am twelve years old. My mother has doubts. She hears a sour note in my father's voice on the phone now. He rants to her about the conspiracy against him, about the enemies of Allah, whose lies are legion. He is full of schemes to get released, and he barks orders at her: *Write to the judge! Call Pakistan! Go to the Egyptian embassy! Are you writing all this down?!* My mother yeses him quietly.

On October first, my father, along with the Blind Sheikh and eight others, is convicted of forty-eight out of fifty charges and sentenced to life plus fifteen years without parole. The murder of Monica Rodriguez Smith's unborn child is included in the sentencing.

After the new round of convictions, we see my father once—at the Metropolitan Correctional Center in New York. My mother is terrified about what will become of her and her children. We are destitute. We have no plans for survival—and no hope of my father ever being a true father, or husband, again. Even now, my father will not admit any guilt. When he goes to hug and kiss my mother, she pulls away for the first time, so repulsed that she thinks she's going to vomit. For many years, she will try to console us by saying that we have a father who loves us. But she will always remember the visit to the

MCC as the day that her own heart finally gave up. My father is shipped off to a series of maximum-security prisons around the country. We can no longer afford to visit, even if we wanted to. My mother barely has the money to pay for my father's collect calls anymore. I don't want to talk to him anyway. What's the point? All he ever says is, "Are you making your prayers? Are you being good to your mother?" And all I want to say is, *Are* you *being good to my mother, Baba? Do you know that she has no money and that she's crying all the time?* But, of course, I'm too scared to say any of this. So my father and I keep having the same pointless conversations, and I twist the springy phone cord tighter and tighter around my hand because I just want it all to stop.

My mother wants it to stop, too. All that matters to her now is her children.

She demands a divorce, and we all change our last name.

We've seen my father for the last time.

ABOVE Zak visiting his father on Rikers Island in 1991.

OPPOSITE Zak visiting his father. Attica Correctional Facility, 1994. In the background: The small house where the family stayed together for the weekend.

8 April 1996
Memphis, Tennessee

I'm free from my father's influence, but my education in violence—its ravages and its pointlessness—is not over, thanks to an awful new school and a vicious stepfather who's about to appear on the horizon. I'm not going to pretend that, as a thirteen-year-old, I've already internalized Martin Luther King, Jr.'s teachings—that my enemies are suffering too, that retaliation is a dead end, and that pain can redeem and transform you. No, I simply hate getting hit. It makes me furious and fills me with self-loathing, and I fight back every single time. But everything I experience contributes to the day when I will finally understand that nonviolence is the only sane, humane response to conflict, whether in the hallways of a high school or on the global stage.

I'll call my new school Queensridge Junior-Senior High. I'm one of the only "white" kids—my whole life I've been considered a Caucasian by minorities, and a minority by Caucasians—and I'm not Southern, so bullies have their choice of reasons to beat me up. Only one teacher tries to protect me. The rest all but encourage it. When my mother calls the police after a particularly violent attack, they refuse to even take a report. The school is a nightmare. There are drugs

changing hands in the hallways. There's gang violence.
One day, during social studies, the teacher steps out
and two students start having sex in the back of the
classroom.

In the middle of all this, my father calls from prison,
sounding angry and agitated. He rushes through the
usual questions with my sister, my brother, and me,
then tells me to put my mother on the phone. She hasn't
spoken to him since the divorce. When I hold out the
receiver, she recoils. I don't know what to do. I make a
pleading face and shake the phone: *Take it. Please, just
take it?* Finally, she relents. For me.

My mother can't even get a word out before my father
launches into his latest scheme to get out of prison.
There's an important Pakistani diplomat visiting
Washington, D.C., he tells her. She must make contact
with him. She must convince him to trade an Israeli
prisoner for *him*.

"A prisoner exchange—it is the only hope," he says.
"You must do this and you *must not fail* like you have
failed before."

My mother is silent.

"Sayyid," she says finally. "I am not your wife
anymore—and I am certainly not your secretary."

For the next few minutes, I sit at the kitchen table
dumbstruck, as my mother tells my father that he has
destroyed our lives, that it sounds like he's *losing his
marbles*, and that she never wants to hear his voice again.
She doesn't say that she suspects he's guilty of everything

he's ever been accused of—maybe because she knows I'm listening. In any case, my father is seething now, and he says something that removes any doubt of his guilt: "I did what I had to do, and you know that very well."

• • •

My mother doesn't outright tell me that my father *is* a murderer after all, but I must suspect it because I get angrier at him with every passing week. After Kahane's death, I could comfort myself with the fact that my father had been found not guilty of murder and that, at worst, he would come home to us a free man in 2012. But by conspiring to bomb the World Trade Center, he has not just participated in a heinous act, but also seen to it that we will never be a family again. *Life plus fifteen without parole.* My father will never play soccer with me again. And he chose that fate himself. He chose terrorism over fatherhood, and hate over love. Forget the fact that our family is more infamous than ever now—the WTC bombing has polluted America's opinions of *all* Muslims. When we're in the station wagon, other drivers notice my mother's headscarf and veil and give her the finger, or swerve at us and try to drive us off the road. When we're shopping, people recoil at the sight of her. People shout at my mother, often in broken English, to *go back to her own country.* And I'm ashamed every time—not because I'm Muslim, but because I can never summon the courage to shout back, "She was born in Pittsburgh, idiot!"

I'm a teenager now, and, even before the WTC bombing, my self-esteem was shot through with holes. The bullying at school is never going to stop, my stomach hurts *all the time*, and I bang my head against my bedroom wall at night for the same reasons that girls my age cut themselves. I think about how easy, how peaceful, it would be to be dead, and now there's this horrible new realization: My father chose terrorism over *me*.

● ● ●

Not long after my father's call, my mother gets a scary, lung-rattling cough that turns into bronchitis. She's sick for so long—and so underwater emotionally—that one night I overhear her praying to Allah for guidance. Two weeks later, there seems to be a parting of the clouds: The wife of our sheikh calls and announces that their family has a friend in New York City who's looking for a wife. Because of everything that's about to happen, I'll change the man's name and call him Ahmed Sufyan.

Ahmed was born in Egypt, like my father. He works in an electronics store, and he's an amateur boxer—lean and wiry, his arms ropy with muscles. Like my mother, Ahmed has three children. And he says he is *also* escaping a dreadful marriage: As he tells it, his ex-wife was a prostitute before he met her, and he'd been forced to divorce her when he found her in her former pimp's house, a crack pipe in her hand and their youngest child in her arms. For two weeks, Ahmed and my mother get to know each other over the phone. He tells her that he considers my father to be a heroic servant of Allah, and that he'd always hoped to meet my family and help us out however he could. My mother invites him to Memphis, so they can talk face-to-face.

The night Ahmed arrives, my mother makes baked chicken, rice, and salad for dinner. I am so starved for a father that I'm ready to love him before he even sits down. He appears to be a good Muslim—he instructs us to pray before we eat—and because he's a boxer I'm already imagining late-night lessons where he teaches me how to fight back at school. I've never had much luck with hope before. But we all deserve a happy chapter, my mother more than anyone. My eyes fill with tears when this man who met my mother three hours ago looks around the table at us and says something that *should* seem ominous: "Don't worry, children. Your father is here now."

By the end of the summer, we've moved back to New Jersey and met Ahmed's kids. After our parents marry, the whole Muslim Brady Bunch shares a motel room in Newark while Ahmed saves enough money to rent an apartment. I'm trying to get along with his family, but it's difficult. Eventually one of his sons and I have a scuffle over what to watch on TV. Ahmed takes his son's side. I've been punished before—my father would sometimes spank me with a flip-flop—but never by someone who enjoyed it and never with a belt buckle.

• • •

Ahmed turns out to be a poor excuse for a Muslim. No, he doesn't drink or eat pork, but he also doesn't fast or make his prayers or invoke Islam at all, unless there's someone he wants to impress or control or hate. He is petty, paranoid, and vengeful. He trusts his own children blindly—particularly the son who lies to him repeatedly—but he lays in wait for the rest of us, desperate to catch us doing something wrong.

We find a place in Elizabeth, New Jersey—a small attic apartment where we live without much in the way of furniture. Ahmed's behavior becomes more and more bizarre. He pretends he's going to work but instead stands outside our building for hours, watching us through the windows. He makes me walk miles to school every morning, and secretly follows me in his car. There's practically no money for food, but he takes his own children out for pizza and brings nothing back for us. One weekend, my brother and I wind up in the emergency room because we're malnourished. The doctor's so furious that he's about to call Child Protective Services when my mother—sick from malnutrition herself—begs him to put down the phone. The episode doesn't bother Ahmed. He thinks I'm disgusting because I'm chubby. He spends an entire two-week period calling me *cow* in Arabic.

Ahmed punishes my brother and me for every infraction, whether real or imagined. He uses his fists, his belt, a hanger. Because he's a boxer and goes to the gym obsessively, his punishments are often full-on beatdowns, and I can tell he's testing different combinations of punches. Ahmed's favorite maneuver, though, is a weird sort of fake-out: First, he rushes at me from across the room, his face full of rage. Then, when I've covered my face with my hands, he jumps in the air and stomps on my unguarded foot.

My mother looks out the window when she can't stand to watch anymore. Ahmed's been so abusive to her that she can hardly think straight. He's convinced her that we've become morally corrupt since my father went to prison, and that only he can redeem us. Once, when she tries to intervene on my behalf, he hits her in the head with a vase.

Ahmed is not a murderer like my father, but within the walls of our apartment—among people he claims to love—he is every inch a terrorist.

●　●　●

When I turn fourteen, I start stealing money from him. First, it's just pocket change. Then it's five- and ten-dollar bills that I find under the mattress while making the bed. Usually, I take the money because there's no food in the house, and there's a Dunkin' Donuts on the way to school. Sometimes, I just want to buy a CD by The Roots like everybody else. It amazes me that Ahmed has no idea I'm stealing from him. Gradually, I get bolder and bolder.

Ahmed, it turns out, knows damn well that I'm stealing. He's just choosing the right moment to pounce.

One morning, I pocket a twenty-dollar bill from under the mattress and buy a cool laser pen. That night Ahmed finally confronts me in my bedroom.

I confess. I apologize. I reach into the top drawer of my dresser where I've been hiding the money. Ahmed has a habit of rooting through our belongings, so I've been unscrewing the bottom of my deodorant and hiding the bills inside.

Ahmed steps closer to me. My room is so tiny that there's barely enough space for the two of us. His proximity is terrifying. But he hasn't laid a hand on me yet. In fact, when he sees me unscrew the deodorant and remove the money, he nods as if he's impressed.

"Sneaky," he says.

He doesn't look angry as much as *overjoyed*, which seems strange—until I realize why.

That night, Ahmed takes me into the master bedroom and beats and interrogates me about the thefts from midnight until well into the next day. He asks me how stupid I think he is. He asks me if I've forgotten whose house I'm living in—if I really imagine, in my puny cow brain, that there's anything that goes on that he's not aware of *before it even happens*. He tells me to take off my shirt, and do one hundred push-ups. As I struggle through them, he kicks me in the stomach and ribs. Later, he whacks my palm with a hanger so many times that, for weeks, I'll have cuts and scabs in the precise shape of the hanger's hook—it will look like a question mark on my hand.

All the while, my mother lies on the sofa in the living room, sobbing. She comes to the bedroom door only once and, before she can even beg Ahmed to stop, he shouts at her, "Nosair would be *disgusted* by the way you raise his children! You are lucky I am here to correct your mistakes!"

I've experimented with bullying myself. Back when I was eleven, there was a new kid in school. He was Asian and, with nothing but stereotypes to rely on, I assumed that all Asians knew martial arts. I thought it would be awesome and Ninja Turtley to do some karate stuff, so I goaded him all day long into fighting me. As it happened, this particular Asian kid *did* know martial arts: He pretended to punch me in the face and, when I ducked, he kicked me in the head. I fled school in tears, but was stopped by the crossing guard, who sent me to the nurse's office, where I was given a frozen peanut butter and jelly sandwich to press against my eye.

All in all, it was a humiliating experience. So it's not until after Ahmed beats me for stealing that I try my hand at bullying again. I'm walking down the hallway at school and come upon a bunch of younger kids playing keep-away with a boy's backpack. The boy is crying. I grab the backpack and slam-dunk it into a trash can. For a moment, the sensation is gratifying. There's no denying that there's a rush to being on the other side of the equation. But then I see a look on the poor, tormented kid's face that I recognize so viscerally—it's bewilderment as much as fear—that I pull the bag out of the garbage and hand it back to him. No one's ever sat me down and taught me what empathy is or why it matters more than power or patriotism or religious faith. But I learn it right there in the hallway: I cannot do what's been done to me.

9   December 1998
Alexandria, Egypt

I'm fifteen the last time Ahmed lays a hand on me. We've moved to Egypt because it's cheaper and because my stepfather has family who can help my mother with us kids. There are six of us living in a two-bedroom apartment in a massive concrete building in a neighborhood called Smouha. The place is dingy and in disrepair. It's also freezing cold now that it's the winter, because the concrete doesn't retain heat. Still, there's a mall nearby and a supermarket under construction. It's not the worst place we've ever lived.

One Saturday, a friend from the neighborhood and I are just messing around in the street, sword fighting with sticks, when Ahmed's son and a bunch of other kids rush over because they think we're really fighting. Some of the kids start throwing rocks at us. Not hard, really—they're just playing. But they get more and more aggressive, so I shout, "Stop!" I'm the oldest one there, and the biggest. Everybody stops. Except for Ahmed's son. He just has to throw *one* more rock—right at my face. It breaks my glasses and cuts my nose. Everybody panics and scatters.

At home, my mother asks what happened.

"Before I tell you," I say, "you have to *swear* that you won't tell Ahmed."

I know that there's no way he'll believe me over his son, and that second prize will be a beating. My mother promises she won't say a word. So I tell her everything, and she sends Ahmed's son to his room as punishment. I'm ecstatic. It's a tiny bit of justice after two and a half years of abuse. That night, while I'm in bed, I hear Ahmed come home from the *masjid*. I hear the tinkle of glass as he drops his keys into a bowl by his bedside. I hear the chiming of hangers as he hangs up his shirt and pants. I hear him do his nightly push-ups—complete with a series of unnecessarily loud grunts. And then I hear my mother do something that breaks my heart: she tells him everything.

Ahmed calls me into their bedroom. He doesn't say a word about what his son has done, though he must see that my glasses have been clumsily taped together and that there's dried blood on the bridge of my nose. What he says is: "Why were you playing with sticks?"

And that question just makes me explode.

Not at Ahmed, but at my mother.

"See!" I shout at her. "This is exactly why I didn't want you to tell him! Because he's just going to blame me—like he always does." I stop for a second. I'm full of indignation, and I feel the need to say just one thing more. "Because he's an *asshole*!"

I take the space heater from the floor, and hurl it at a wall. The cord throws off a few sparks as it's ripped from the socket, and the bars of the heater rattle and make a loud *thong*.

I walk out of their bedroom and go down to the
kitchen, crying and screaming. I'm out of control in a
way that scares even me. I'm punching the kitchen door
over and over again when I hear Ahmed storming down
the hall after me. I know what's coming. The moment he
enters the kitchen, I drop to the floor and curl into a ball
as he begins to pummel me with his fists. I'm just going to
take it like I always do.

Suddenly, my mother rushes into the room. She
screams for Ahmed to stop. He's so shocked that she's
come to my defense that she manages to push him away.
She helps me to my feet. She smoothes my hair, and the
three of us just stand there in the kitchen, panting.

My mother whispers, "I'm so sorry, Z."

Ahmed can't believe what he's hearing.

"Oh, she's so sorry!" he says, disgusted. "I am only
doing what Nosair would do—what you are too weak to
do yourself!"

My hands are on my knees—I'm wearing my
bedclothes, a long gown called a *jalabiyah*—and I'm
trying to catch my breath when Ahmed punches me
again. An uppercut, perfected in the gym. My mother
steps between us. But Ahmed just won't stop. He jabs to
the left and right of her head. He couldn't care less if he
hits her, which enrages me, so I do something that shocks
the hell out of Ahmed, my mother, *and* me: I punch him
back.

It's a wild swing. I don't even hit him. Still, for half a
second, Ahmed's eyes pop wide with fear. He stalks out

of the kitchen, never to touch me again. It's a victory, but a short-lived one. He just starts beating my younger brother even more.

● ● ●

After New Year's, I accept a collect call from my father, who's now at a "supermax"—short for super-maximum security—prison in California. I rarely talk to him anymore, and I can tell by his voice that he's surprised when he's put through. I remember the time my mother let him have it on the phone, and I want to have some catharsis of my own. I want to tell him how crappy our lives have become since he decided that other people's deaths were more important than his own family's lives. I want to scream into the phone. I want to lose control for once because he should know the price we're paying for his crimes. I'm never going to see him again anyway. He's in prison. For life. He has no control over me. He can't hurt me—and he *certainly* can't help me.

But, as always, I can't get the anger out. I just sob into the phone. My father pretends not to notice. He asks me blandly if I'm making my prayers and being good to my mother.

10 July 1999
Philadelphia, Pennsylvania

By the time I'm sixteen, I've spent quite some time
hiding behind the surname Ebrahim. It's been like
an invisibility cloak, and, lately at least, it's been
working: None of my new friends know that I was born
a Nosair. My family's Egyptian experiment has failed.
We've moved back to the States. And—I don't know if
it's because I've pulled further away from my father,
or because I no longer live in fear of my stepfather's
violence—I'm starting to feel hopeful and buoyant for the
first time since my mother woke me up to tell me there'd
been an "accident." I decide to take a leap of faith and tell
my two best friends who I really am. I tell them I'm the
son of El-Sayyid Nosair.

I confess to my friend Orlando first. We're on a class
trip, sitting on a bench in the courtyard of a museum.
The name Nosair means nothing to him, so I take a deep
breath and explain. I tell him that my father murdered
a rabbi named Meir Kahane and helped orchestrate
the attack on the World Trade Center. Orlando looks
incredulous. He's so shocked by the horror of it all that all
he can do is laugh. He laughs so hard that he falls off the
bench. He does not judge me.

The second person I tell is my friend Suboh. We work

together at a supermarket in a bad neighborhood and, since he's old enough to drive, he drops me off at home when we're done for the day. Suboh is Palestinian. He knows the name El-Sayyid Nosair and the dark things it stands for. I tell him that Orlando is the only other person in the world whom I've told about my father—or that I plan to tell. We're sitting in Suboh's car outside my house. He looks at me and nods. I'm afraid of his reaction. The windows rattle as trucks go by. When Suboh finally speaks, he does in fact rebuke me, though not in the way I'd feared: "You told Orlando before you told *me*?" I feel a rush of relief. If my friends don't blame me for my father's sins, then maybe, slowly, I can stop blaming myself. I feel as if I've been carrying something enormous and heavy, and finally put it down.

•   •   •

In 2001, we pick up and move yet again. My sister has married and moved away. The rest of us head to Tampa, where Ahmed thinks he can find work. Yes, Ahmed is still around—he's like mold in the walls we can never get rid of. But it's becoming clear that he can't tell me what to think any more than my father can. His reign of terror is getting pathetic, and it ends the day he insists my brother and I get summer jobs.

We're thrilled at the thought of having some money, even if Ahmed will take half of it to pay bills. It's hiring season at Busch Gardens, so we troop down

to the theme park and fill out applications and sit for
interviews with a mass of other sunburned teens.
We expect nothing. Miraculously, we both get hired.
I'm going to be a Rhino Rally guide, which is beyond
awesome: *Plunge into the deepest heart of Africa! On
our guided tour, you'll experience all the excitement of
a safari and come face-to-face with some of the planet's
most majestic animals. Come on! Let's aim for adventure!*
My brother will be working Congo River Rapids, which
he insists is even more beyond awesome: *Get ready for
the wildest river ride ever! Once you've climbed aboard
a giant Busch Gardens raft, you'll shoot perilous rapids,
pass under pounding waterfalls, and investigate the
strangest of water caves. What are you waiting for? Let's
get wet!*

Some teenagers might yawn at the thought of working
at a theme park, but my brother and I are elated. We
are babbling, high-fiving idiots in Pittsburgh Penguins
T-shirts. In Tampa, there's sunshine, there's water
everywhere, there's salt in the air. The world is opening
up to us at last. For years, we've been on the run from our
father's legacy, outcasts, terrified. For years, Ahmed has
beaten us and *watched* us in such a creepy way that we've
never felt safe. But now, my brother and I will lead safaris
and river rides. We will go somewhere that Ahmed can't
follow. The only way to get into Busch Gardens is to work
there or buy a ticket. If he wants to spy on us now, it's
going to cost him fifty bucks.

And this is how I finally, finally, finally get the chance

to discover life on my own terms: my father is locked in, and my stepfather is locked out.

• • •

I'm eighteen now, and over the summer in Tampa, all the teenage rites of passage line up before me. I go to parties for the first time. I get drunk for the first time. I pretend I'm going to buy a soda and *actually* just smoke a cigarette in the 7-Eleven parking lot. I buy a car. *A car.* The quintessential symbol of freedom! I mean, it's a terrible, terrible car—an old Ford Taurus with stickers and decals that won't come off. Still, I worship it so much that I lie in bed at night thinking about it, like it's my girlfriend or something. Truthfully, my bad-boy experiments are all timid and short-lived. My real rebellion is that I'm starting to question everything my father stands for. From the moment I put on my Rhino Rally safari suit, I meet tourists and coworkers of every description, which is so liberating that I can hardly put the feeling into words. I'm taking every fundamentalist lie I was ever told about people—about nations and wars and religions—and holding it up to the light.

When I was a kid, I never questioned what I heard at home or at school or at the mosque. Bigotry just slipped into my system along with everything else: *Alexander Graham Bell invented the telephone. Pi equals 3.14. All Jews are evil, and homosexuality is an abomination. Paris is the capital of France.* They all sounded like facts. Who was I to differentiate? I was made to fear people who were different and kept away from them as much as possible for my own "protection." Bigotry is such a maddeningly perfect circle—I never got close enough to find out if I should fear them in the first place.

Because my father was obsessed with the Middle East, I was constantly reminded that Jews were villains, end of discussion. And gays? When I was fifteen, three Afghan men were found guilty of sodomy, and the Taliban decreed that they were going to bury them under a pile of rocks and then use a tank to push a wall down on top of them. The Taliban's version of mercy was that if the men were still alive after thirty minutes, their lives would be spared.

This was the sort of dogma that had been seeping into my brain since I was born, and it was only being reinforced by the strains of anti-Semitism and homophobia in American culture. Lately, though, there'd been an unlikely new voice chipping away at the lies: Jon Stewart.

I always loved *The Daily Show* with Craig Kilborn, and when they announced that Stewart was taking over, I was indignant in the way only a teenager can be: *Who is this guy? Bring back Kilborn!* But, in Tampa, I watch Stewart obsessively and insist my mother sit on the couch alongside me. Stewart's humor is like a gateway drug. He makes it seem cool to probe and to question and to care—about the antiwar movement, about gay rights, about everything. The man *hates* dogma. I've gulped down so much so-called wisdom in my life that Stewart is a revelation. Frankly, he's as close to a reasoning and humane father figure as I'll ever get. I stay up late just waiting for him to decipher the world for me, and he helps adjust a lot of the faulty wiring in my brain. It seems only fitting that my new role model is Jewish.

• • •

The Rhino Rally job is phenomenal. A total blast. It turns out that, buried beneath my self-doubt, I'm a bit of a ham. This becomes clear when I put on the headset microphone and get behind the wheel of the Land Rover. All guides follow the same basic script, but we can improvise as much as we like, as long as nobody breaks an arm or files a complaint. For each tour, I pick a "navigator" to sit beside me. If anybody wants to do it *too* badly—there's always some kid whose hand rockets into the air before I'm even done explaining the job—I never pick them. I want people who are friendly and unsure of themselves and who look as if they can take some teasing. It never occurs to me to care what God they pray to—although, to be honest, if they're wearing a Philadelphia Flyers jersey, forget it. I'm not perfect.

One day in August, I load eighteen tourists into the Rover and announce that my regular navigator has unfortunately been eaten by a crocodile ("We may actually see part of him in the pond a little later") and ask if anyone would like to volunteer. The usual hands start waving. Everybody else starts poking around in their backpacks and handbags to avoid eye contact. One man, a slightly tubby, fiftysomething dad with a fanny pack is actively blushing. So I step up, hand him a headset, and say, "Please?" Dread passes over his face, but his children start chanting, "Do it, Abba! Do it!" and I know I've got him. He takes the headset and the tour group roars its approval, which causes him to blush even more deeply. Once he's settled into the navigator's seat, I ask him some questions for the crowd's benefit.

"Hello, sir. What's your name?"

"Tomer."

"Excellent. You can call me Z. Where are you from?"

"Israel."

"Very good. Tell me, Tomer, do you have any experience warding off lions, binding leg wounds, or making soup from tree bark?"

"No, I really don't."

"None at all?"

"It, uh—it hasn't come up."

"Okay, hopefully we can work around it. We're going to pass over a pretty rickety bridge, though. How long can you hold your breath under water?"

"I don't know how to swim."

"Weird. Those were actually my regular navigator's last words."

"Seriously?"

"No, his last words were actually, 'Help me, Z! Why

are you driving away?!' But you get the idea. Tomer, I don't mean to be rude, but you seem really unqualified to be a navigator. I'm kinda surprised you volunteered."

"My watch has a compass on it."

"You know what? That's good enough for me. Let's hear it for Tomer, everybody!"

The crowd laughs and claps, Tomer's kids louder than anyone, and we're off.

• • •

Some version of that scene plays out every day at Rhino Rally, with every conceivable kind of person sitting in the navigator's seat. It's amazing how much you can learn about somebody when you survive the rain forest *and* the savannah together, when the bridge you're crossing suddenly splits apart and your vehicle falls into the river and floats away on a raft of miraculous lifesaving logs. The flood of people, people, and people into my life is intoxicating. I walk around Busch Gardens with my head literally held higher because I know people *who are not like me*. I've got incontrovertible proof that my father raised me on lies. Bigotry is stupid. It only works if you never walk out your door.

During my breaks from Rhino Rally, I start hanging out at Busch Gardens's Middle Eastern rock show, Moroccan Roll. (I've always loved the idea of being onstage. I got a part in a high school production of *Bye Bye Birdie* once, though Ahmed wouldn't let me take it.) I go to the show so often, in fact, that I make friends with a Muslim trumpet player named Yamin. Through him I meet two dancers, Marc and Sean, who are gay. I'm reticent around them at first. I have no experience with gay men and, I'm ashamed to admit it, I judge them. Because of what I've been taught, it's like there's a sign over their heads flashing the words BAD INFLUENCE! BAD INFLUENCE! Maybe they don't notice that I'm standoffish. Maybe they pity me for my small-mindedness. Or maybe they're just giving me a free pass because I'm friends with Yamin. In any case, they are nothing but genuine and nonjudgmental with me. They let me babble about Rhino Rally, they don't laugh when I say I secretly love to sing, they try (and fail) to teach me a few dance moves. Their sheer niceness breaks me down. I've been bullied for so long that I'm a sucker for kindness.

It's around this time that I come home in my Rhino Rally outfit one night and tell my mother that, despite all of my father's and Ahmed's proclamations, I'm going to try trusting the world. My mother has never made ugly comments about people, but she's been subject to even more dogma than I have over the years. It's now that she says those six words that I will build the rest of my life around: "I'm so sick of hating people."

•   •   •

Then suddenly, amazingly, we are free of Ahmed. Even my mother is free. She doesn't leave Ahmed in a fit of rage—she doesn't tell him that he's a hateful human being and that there's no Muslim paradise waiting for him. She's too weary, too beaten down for that. Still, leaving him at all is a triumph in my book. She packs up and returns to Pittsburgh to care for her own mother, who has had a series of brain aneurysms.

I've only met my grandmother a few times in my life because she was so appalled when my mother converted to Islam. She apparently meant it when she said my mother wasn't welcome at her house wearing *some goddamn scarf* on her head. For my mother, though, love and loyalty transcend everything. And it turns out that, in the midst of my grandmother's decline, a strange, fortuitous thing has happened. If you ever need proof that bigotry is nothing but a trick of the mind, here it is: Because of her strokes, my grandmother has forgotten, utterly and in an instant, that she hates my mother's religion and abhors my mother for choosing it. And prejudice is not the only bad habit my grandmother's brain has let go of: She's also forgotten that she had smoked for fifty years.

•   •   •

Before the summer ends, some of my Busch Gardens buddies and I take a long lunch and check out a roller coaster called Montu. The ride's named after an ancient god of war who was half man and half falcon. It's in a part of the park called Egypt, which strikes my funny bone in just the right way. It rises like a sea monster up over

palm trees and Middle Eastern–themed shops and faux
sandstone ruins covered in Arabic. (The Arabic cracks
me up: it's all gibberish.) My new friends and I climb into
the coaster. Nobody can shut up. They're arguing about
what Montu's coolest feature is: is it the *seven totally
intense inversions*? Is it the wild-ass *zero-G roll*? Is it the
out-friggin'-rageous *Immelman loop*? They can't decide.
They want me to cast the tie-breaking vote, but I have no
idea what they're talking about because there's one more
thing we'd never experienced in our Islamic bubble—real
live roller coasters!—and I'm scared out of my mind.

   We're towed up to the first crest and released into what
feels like a free fall. For a solid minute, I cannot even
open my eyes. When I do, I see my friends' faces. They
are shining with happiness. I gaze out over Egypt. The
Serengeti plain. The parking lot. Then we hurtle into the
zero-G roll at sixty miles an hour, and there are three
questions pinging in my mind: 1) Are my shoes going to
fall off? 2) If I throw up, will the vomit travel up or down?
and 3) Why didn't anyone take just a couple of seconds
out from telling me who I was born to hate and mention,
even in passing, that roller coasters are *the coolest things
in the world*?

   My mind flashes back to my very first memory: my
father and I spinning in the giant tea cups at Kennywood
Amusement Park, in Pennsylvania. I was only three
at the time, so I really just remember flashes of light
and bursts of color. One moment does come back,

though—my father laughing, standing up in the tea cup and shouting a familiar prayer: "O Allah, protect me and deliver me to my destination!"

My father lost his way—but that didn't stop me from finding mine.

11 Epilogue

I've written so much about prejudice in this book because turning someone into a bigot is the first step in turning him into a terrorist. You find someone vulnerable— someone who's lost his confidence, his income, his pride, his agency. Someone who feels humiliated by life. And then you isolate him. You fill him with fear and fury, and you see to it that he regards anybody who's different as a faceless target—a silhouette at a shooting range like Calverton—rather than a human being. But even people who've been raised on hate since birth, people whose minds have been warped and weaponized, can make a choice about who they want to be. And they can be extraordinary advocates for peace, precisely because they've seen the effects of violence, discrimination, and disenfranchisement firsthand. People who have been victimized can understand more deeply than anyone how little the world needs more victims.

I know that systemic poverty, fanaticism, and lack of education make the kind of transformation I'm describing a staggering long shot in some parts of the world. I also know that not everyone has the moral fire of Gandhi, Nelson Mandela, or Martin Luther King, Jr.—I certainly don't—and that not everybody can convert suffering into resolve. But I'm convinced that empathy is more powerful than hate and that our lives should be dedicated to making it go viral.

Empathy, peace, nonviolence—they may seem like quaint tools in the world of terror that my father helped create. But, as many have written, using nonviolence to resolve conflicts doesn't mean being passive. It doesn't mean embracing victimhood, or letting aggressors run riot. It doesn't even mean giving up the fight, not exactly. What it means is humanizing your opponents, recognizing the needs and fears you share with them, and working toward reconciliation rather than revenge. The longer I stare at this famous quote by Gandhi, the more I love how steely and hardcore it is: "There are many causes I would die for. There is not a single cause I would kill for." Escalation cannot be our only response to aggression, no matter how hardwired we are to hit back and hit back harder. The late counterculture historian Theodore Roszak once put it this way: "People try nonviolence for a week, and when it 'doesn't work,' they go back to violence, which hasn't worked for centuries."

• • •

I stopped taking my father's calls when I was eighteen. Every so often, I'll get an e-mail from the prison in Illinois saying that he would like to initiate correspondence. But I've learned that even that leads nowhere good. My father's been appealing his convictions forever—he thinks the State infringed on

his civil rights during the investigation—so one time I
e-mailed him and asked, flat-out, whether he murdered
Rabbi Kahane, and whether he participated in the plot
to attack the World Trade Center in 1993. I told him, *I'm
your son and I need to hear it from you.* He answered me
with an indecipherable, high-flown metaphor that had
more twists and turns than the roller coaster at Busch
Gardens. It made him seem desperate and grasping. Not
to mention guilty.

Kahane's assassination was not just hateful, but a
failure as anything other than simple murder. My father
intended to shut the rabbi up and to bring glory unto
Allah. What he *actually* did was to bring shame and
suspicion onto all Muslims, and to inspire more pointless
and cowardly acts of violence. On New Year's Eve in
2000, the rabbi's youngest son and daughter-in-law were
killed—and five of their six children wounded—when
Palestinian gunmen fired machine guns into the family's
van as they made their way home. Another family
destroyed by hate. I felt sick with sadness when I read
about it.

I felt sicker still on 9/11. I sat watching the footage in
our living room in Tampa, forcing myself to absorb the
unfathomable horror of the attack—and struggling with
the devastating feeling that I was somehow complicit by
blood. Of course, the pain I felt was nothing compared to
the pain of the true victims and their families. My heart
still breaks for them.

One of the many upsides to not speaking to my father

anymore is that I've never had to listen to him pontificate about the vile events that took place on September 11th. He must have regarded the destruction of the Twin Towers as a great victory for Islam—maybe even as the culmination of the work he and the Blind Sheikh and Ramzi Yousef began years earlier with the yellow Ryder van.

For what it's worth—and I'm not sure what it *is* worth at this point—my father now claims to support a peaceful solution in the Middle East. He also claims to abhor the killing of innocents, and he admonishes jihadists to *think of their families*. He said all this in an interview with the *Los Angeles Times* in 2013. I hope his change of heart is genuine, though it comes too late for the innocents who were murdered and for my family, which was torn apart. I don't pretend to know what my father believes anymore. I just know that I spent too many years caring.

As for me, I'm no longer a Muslim and I no longer believe in God. It broke my mother's heart when I told her, which, in turn, broke mine. My mother's world is held together by her faith in Allah. What defines *my* world is love for my family and friends, the moral conviction that we must all be better to one another and to the generations that will come after us, and the desire to undo some of the damage my father has done in whatever small ways I can. There's one remaining vestige of my own religious education. Whenever I read online about some new act of evil, I instinctively hope against hope that it isn't the work of Muslims—the many peaceful followers of Islam have already paid a high enough price for the actions of the fundamentalist fringe. Otherwise, I put people before gods. I respect believers of all kinds and work to promote interfaith dialogue, but my whole life I've seen religion used as a weapon, and I'm putting all weapons down.

● ● ●

In April 2012, I had the surreal experience of giving a speech in front of a couple hundred federal agents at the FBI headquarters in Philadelphia. The Bureau wanted to build a better rapport with the Muslim community, and the agent in charge of the campaign had heard me advocate for peace at his son's school, so there I was—feeling honored, but nervous. It was a daunting crowd. I started with a joke ("I'm not used to seeing so many of you at once—usually I deal with you two at a time"), which was met with confused silence and then a pretty good laugh, for which I will be forever grateful. I proceeded to tell my story, and to offer myself up as proof that it is possible to shut one's ears to hatred and violence and simply choose peace.

After my talk, I asked if there were any questions, and there weren't. That seemed unusual, but maybe the FBI agents were too nervous to raise their hands? Anyway, I said, "Thank you very much for having me," and the crowd clapped and began to disperse. And then something nice happened, which has always stayed with me: A handful of agents formed a line to shake my hand.

The first few agents offered polite words and firm grips. The third one, a woman, had been crying.

"You probably don't remember me—and there's no reason you should," she said. "But I was one of the agents that worked on your father's case." She paused awkwardly, which made my heart go out to her. "I always wondered what happened to the children of El-Sayyid Nosair," she continued. "I was afraid that you'd followed in his path."

I'm proud of the path I've chosen. And I think I speak for my brother and sister when I say that rejecting our father's extremism both saved our lives and made our lives worth living.

To answer the agent's question, here is what happened to the children of El-Sayyid Nosair:

We are not his children anymore.

ACKNOWLEDGMENTS

To my best friend, Sharon. Words cannot adequately express all that you've given me. You've been everything. Saying "This wouldn't have been possible without you" is an understatement. Thanks, buddy.

Thank you to Robin and Warren, our dynamic "god parents," who provided us with amazing guidance and their ridiculous wealth of knowledge.

To my mother, who instilled in me a love of reading that benefits me every single day. I don't know how you got us through it all. To my loving sister, for always being there. To my brother: the bond we've shared since we were kids will be with me forever. You are the coolest person I know.

Thank you to Frank, Vera, and Frankie.

Thank you to my dear friends in Pittsburgh—Holly and Doug, Mike and Chad, Mark and Tracy, Mike and Betsy, Jeff, Kate, Kaitlin and Alisa, Knut, Cathy and Colin, and Mike and Jules, for your amazing support, and for making me realize how big my family really is. Go Steelers!

Thanks to my Philly friends—Jasmine, and my oldest friends Orlando, Jose, and Suboh. Bill and Cathy for having my back, Special Agent JJ, Alexander and Fin (even though you're Flyers fans), JDKC, Laura V, Marilyn and Elaine, Rabbi Mike, Alex, Rabbi Elliott S., Dave, Pastor Scott H., Brian, Lisa, Pod, DC Jenny, Colleen and Michael, Bob, Heather and Bill, and to Charlie, who always said I needed to do a TED Talk.

I would like to convey my gratefulness to those who supported me throughout my journey: Emily, Sarah, Martina, Jesse, Kathleen, Barbara, Danielle, Marianne, Masa, Todd, Mary Lowell, Michael, Troy and Abed, and to the many people not mentioned who gave me strength and courage along the way.

An enormous thank-you to Jeff Giles. You have been a pleasure to work with, and I'm so thankful for your help with crafting my thoughts into a coherent format. I would like to express special gratitude to Michelle Quint for her positive energy and editorial expertise. My deepest thanks and appreciation to Deron, Alex, June, Ellyn, and everyone at TED for believing in my message. Much appreciation to Carla Sacks for her guidance. Finally, I am very grateful to Chris Anderson for believing that I would not crumble under the pressure of opening for Bill Gates and Sting.

Thank you all.

ABOUT THE AUTHORS

ZAK EBRAHIM was born in Pittsburgh, Pennsylvania on March 24, 1983, the son of an Egyptian industrial engineer and an American schoolteacher. When Ebrahim was seven, his father shot and killed the founder of the Jewish Defense League, Rabbi Meir Kahane. From behind bars Ebrahim's father, El-Sayyid Nosair, co-masterminded the 1993 bombing of the World Trade Center. Ebrahim spent the rest of his childhood moving from city to city, hiding his identity from those who knew of his father. He now dedicates his life to speaking out against terrorism and spreading his message of peace and nonviolence. In 2013, he participated in TED's talent search in New York City, and was selected to speak at the main TED Conference the following year. His TED Talk was the inspiration for this book.

A portion of the earnings the author received to write this book have been donated to Tuesday's Children, a nonprofit organization helping communities affected by terrorism around the world.

Learn more about Tuesday's Children: www.tuesdayschildren.org

JEFF GILES is a journalist and novelist based in New York. He has written for *The New York Times Book Review*, *Rolling Stone*, and *Newsweek*, and served as a top editor at *Entertainment Weekly*. His first novel for young adults will be published by Bloomsbury in 2016.

WATCH ZAK EBRAHIM'S TED TALK

Zak Ebrahim, author of *The Terrorist's Son*, spoke at the TED Conference in 2014. His 9-minute talk, available for free at TED.com, was the inspiration for *The Terrorist's Son*.

go.ted.com/ebrahim

PHOTO: JAMES DUNCAN DAVIDSON

RELATED TALKS ON TED.COM

Scilla Elworthy: *Fighting with nonviolence*
go.ted.com/scilla_elworthy

In this wise and soulful talk, peace activist Scilla Elworthy maps out the skills we need—as nations and individuals—to fight extreme force without using force in return.

Aicha el-Wafi & Phyllis Rodriguez: *The mothers who forged forgiveness, friendship*
go.ted.com/two_mothers

Two mothers have a powerful friendship born of unthinkable loss. One woman's son was killed in the World Trade Center attacks on September 11, 2001; the other woman's son was convicted of a role in those attacks and is serving a life sentence.

Shaka Senghor: *Why your worst deeds don't define you*
go.ted.com/shaka_senghor

In 1991, Shaka Senghor shot and killed a man. Jailed for second degree murder, that could have been the end of his story. Instead, it was the beginning of a journey toward redemption.

Maz Jobrani: *Did you hear the one about the Iranian-American?*
go.ted.com/maz_jobrani

A founding member of the Axis of Evil Comedy Tour, standup comic Maz Jobrani riffs on the challenges and conflicts of being Iranian-American.